Andean Journeys:
A Bilingual Anthology of
Contemporary Bolivian Poetry

Andean Journeys:
A Bilingual Anthology of
Contemporary Bolivian Poetry

Edited by Ronald Haladyna

Introduction, Translations, Bibliographies,
and Notes by the Editor

Order this book online at www.trafford.com
or email orders@trafford.com

Most Trafford titles are also available at major online book retailers.

Printed in the United States of America.

ISBN: 978-1-4269-9604-7 (sc)
ISBN: 978-1-4269-9605-4 (hc)
ISBN: 978-1-4269-9606-1 (e)

Library of Congress Control Number: 2011917064

Trafford rev. 05/08/2012

Trafford
PUBLISHING www.trafford.com

North America & international
toll-free: 1 888 232 4444 (USA & Canada)
phone: 250 383 6864 ✦ fax: 812 355 4082

For Ma Jo,
who vicariously
travels the world,
even to Bolivia.

Contents

PREFACE

Andean Journeys: A Bilingual Anthology of Contemporary Bolivian Poetry is the fourth in a series devoted to bringing works of outstanding Latin American poets to English-speaking nations. As in the case of the anthologies devoted to the poetry of Uruguay, Paraguay, and Ecuador, the objective here is to bring long-overdue recognition to outstanding poets who are virtually unknown outside of their own countries.

Latin American narrative writers—Vargas Llosa, García Márquez, Allende, Fuentes, Bolaño, to name just a few—have achieved worldwide acclaim and readership in the past quarter century (or even longer), but this has not been the case for Latin American poets, especially for those of countries such as the ones being featured in these four anthologies. In North America, for instance, it's unlikely anyone in literary circles could identify, for example, a current Bolivian poet; even more telling is that most university professors and students specializing in Latin-American literature would be hard pressed to rattle off the names of current South-American poets. The reasons for the anonymity of so many of these poets are varied, and some are familiar: narrative literature is more popular than poetry; it is more abundantly available; it is reviewed much more in national and international media; poetry is more 'difficult' to read; so much of poetry in Latin-American countries has not been translated; and it has not been translated because scant attention has been devoted to identifying poets whose works merit translation.

This last reason, in fact, has been my motivation for these anthologies. At a time when an ever-increasing stream of contemporary South-American poetry is being written and published, commensurate research and criticism of these works has not kept pace in South America, much less in other continents. This lack of guidance by academics has not helped distinguish more noteworthy poets from lesser ones. The goal of this anthology is to help create this filter and offer, as it were, a guide to outstanding contemporary poets of Bolivia.

As in the case of the previous anthologies, my Bolivian selection has been swayed by mature, dedicated poets who have a sustained and recognized bibliography of published books of poetry during the past twenty-five years; whose poems have been included in national and international Spanish-language anthologies; who have received favorable recognition by peers and critics, as well as in reviews and interviews in national news media; who have received literary awards within and outside of Bolivia; who, for the most part, are still active as poets; and finally, whose poetry has appealed to me and seemed translatable. Gathered here is an array of poets representing different 'generations,' as well as poems displaying diverse styles, themes, imagination, ideas, and language. A selection of poets representing an entire country is always controversial; 'unpardonable' exclusions are regrettable, but inevitable. In some cases, poets declined participation; others were inaccessible; others didn't quite fulfill the criteria I had established.

For readers unfamiliar with Bolivia, I have provided an introduction which briefly covers the country's unique geography, economy, history/politics, and society. The introduction is not intended to explain why the poets write the way they do, but much of the poetry does allude to these components of the Bolivian reality. This anthology is intended for a general reading public, but it is especially intended for academics. For that reason, I have included a short biographical introduction to each poet, followed by an extensive bibliography of primary and secondary sources. Because of the paucity of academic research and criticism, many of the bibliographical entries included here consist of reviews of books, interviews with the poets, and occasionally more serious analysis. Nevertheless, these entries are offered in the spirit of an initial orientation and an incentive for those so inclined to pursue research on this fertile area of letters.

It should be noted that I have made no attempt in my introductions to characterize, analyze, classify, or otherwise evaluate the poets selected in these anthologies. My evaluation of them, in effect, has been limited to my selecting them as credible representatives of recent Bolivian poetry. Every reading by every reader of poetry is unique, subjective, and valid insofar as it is shaped by the individual life experience, expectations, and imagination of each reader. It becomes even more meaningful when readers compare their views with those of other readers.

In the same spirit of the preceding anthologies, I again signal that there is no canon of contemporary Bolivian poets; but I hope this project will provide a meaningful step toward opening a discussion of such a canon. Poets excluded from this anthology by no means should be excluded from such a discussion.

This book has been long in the making: it started with a sabbatical leave in 1998 when I briefly met a few Bolivian poets and proposed putting together an anthology similar to the ones I had started for Paraguay and Uruguay. It wasn't until my return for several months in 2008 when I was able to carry out extensive research. I was fortunate to find most of the poets I selected in La Paz and Cochabamba.

This anthology could not have been carried to fruition without the generous support of a sabbatical leave and a Research Development Grant from Ferris State University. I also wish to thank Francisco Azuela and Jorge Campero for their help in contacting poets, identifying resources and for their kind hospitality. Not to be forgotten are the librarians of the Simón Patiño Foundation in Cochabamba, and Paola of the Centro de Documentación en Artes y Literaturas Latinoamericanas (CEDOAL) in La Paz for providing me comfortable reading rooms and access to virtually all the needed materials. Both libraries are unparalleled in literary holdings and service in Bolivia.

INTRODUCTION:

CONTEXTUALIZING BOLIVIAN POETRY

Readers in English-speaking countries may not be acquainted with Bolivia, let alone with the poets and the poetry that this anthology presents. This brief introduction to Bolivia merely serves as a backdrop to help situate and understand some basic information about this remote country, so that it won't feel so remote. As in the case of Uruguay, Paraguay and Ecuador—the settings of the three previous anthologies of this series—Bolivia does not often make news in international media, unless it has to do with a natural disaster or political upheaval.

Familiarity with the poets' milieu—especially if it is a distant one—does not necessarily provide readers with special insights into their poetics, intentions, or mystique, any more than biographical data should. However, it will help make clear that these poets, in spite of the vast diversity of themes, styles, language, images, and perspectives, are nevertheless products of very similar circumstances. In fact, most of the poets included here gravitate to two intellectual hubs of Bolivia—La Paz and Cochabamba—and most of them know (of) each other and each other's works. This introduction, then, is intended to familiarize readers with at least a portion of the same background of Bolivia with which the selected poets are already familiar.

GEOGRAPHY

The Plurinational State of Bolivia (its official name) is a stunningly beautiful country, with a wide variety of geographical features and climates in what some would describe as the Tibet of the Americas. Bolivia (as we shall call it) is a medium-sized country—424,162 square miles, about three-quarters the size of Alaska—close to the geographic middle of South America: bordering Brazil to the north and east, Paraguay and Argentina to the south, and Peru and Chile to the west. Although it has access to the Atlantic Ocean via the Paraguay River, Bolivia is considered a land-locked country.

Except for its lack of coastlines, Bolivia resembles Peru in significant geographical features. The most prominent is the Andean region, extending from Peru through western and central Bolivia and on to Chile and Argentina. This region comprises about thirteen per cent of the country's territory and consists of the 'altiplano' (a high tableland averaging about 13,000' above sea level), which includes the Salar de Uyuni, (the world's largest salt flat), and the Andean cordillera, with many volcanic mountains—Sajama, Illampu, Illimani, Ancohuma, and Parinacota—all rising over 20,000' in elevation. Descending from the altiplano toward the east, the sub-Andean region covers about twenty-eight per cent of the country's territory and is comprised of tropical and sub-tropical valleys, steep river canyons called 'yungas' that descend from the Andes, and forests with exuberant vegetation. Coming further down from the sub-Andes, is the region of the alluvial plains—about 59 per cent of Bolivian territory—a mostly flat land covered with grasslands, jungle, and rainforests.

Nestled between Perú and Bolivia, Lake Titicaca is the highest navigable lake in the world, and the largest single body of water accessible to Bolivia. The continental divide, which runs along the length of the Andes, gives birth to four major river basins, one into the Pacific Ocean, and three eventually reaching the Atlantic. There are over 270 principal rivers, originating in the Andean and sub-Andean regions and traversing the country in virtually all directions.

As might be expected with such extremes in elevation so close to the equator, the climate in Bolivia varies dramatically: in the mountains and the altiplano, cool weather prevails with sub-freezing temperatures common at night, and even snow in the higher reaches; in the sub-tropics, temperatures are moderate year round; and in tropical areas, they are hot and steamy. Summer (a.k.a. rainy season) runs from November through March, and winter (dry season) from April through October.

Bolivia is a young nation: of its 10,118,000 population (July, 2011 est.), 34 per cent are under the age of fifteen. Although Bolivia's territory is approximately the size of Spain and France together, it has only about eight per cent of the two European nations' combined population. About sixty per cent of the population is urban, concentrated in its principal cities: Santa Cruz (1,600,000); El Alto (950,000); La Paz (the de-facto capital, 835,000); Cochabamba (618,000); Sucre (the official capital, 284,000); and Oruro (216,000).

ECONOMY

In spite of impressive improvements in its economy in recent years, Bolivia continues to be the poorest and least developed country in South America. In 2010, Bolivia's per capita GNI was $1,790 (ranked by the World Bank 158 of 213 countries in the world), ahead only of Haiti ($650) in the western hemisphere. Over thirty per cent of the population lives below the poverty line (defined as living on less than the international standard of US$2.00 daily).

In agriculture, Bolivia produces soybeans, coffee, coca, cotton, corn, sugarcane, rice, potatoes, and timber, and its principle industries are mining, smelting, petroleum, food and beverages, tobacco, handicrafts, and clothing. Its primary export commodities include natural gas, soybeans, crude petroleum, zinc ore, and tin.

Because the manufacturing base is weak, Bolivia imports petroleum products, plastics, paper, aircraft and parts, foods, automobiles, insecticides, and consumer goods. Bolivia's chief partners in trade are (in order) Brazil, Japan, Argentina, the United States, and Peru. An enormous gas duct was built from eastern Bolivia to Brazil, the principal buyer of Bolivian natural gas and crude oil. Bolivian commerce has suffered greatly because of its land-locked status since the War of the Pacific (1879-1883), when it lost part of its territory including coastline and Arica, a port on the Pacific Ocean.

Due to Bolivia's non-compliance with counter-narcotic provisions of the Andean Trade Promotion and Drug Eradication Act (ATPDEA), in 2008, the United States prohibited the duty-free importation of Bolivian products, a ban that continues today. President Evo Morales has repeatedly affirmed Bolivia's right to cultivate coca (he was a former coca grower) and distribute it. Bolivia is estimated to be the third-largest cultivator of coca (after Colombia and Perú), and has been a transit country for Peruvian and Colombian cocaine destined for other countries in South America and Europe. Nevertheless, the United States remains a trade partner of Bolivia for non-restrictive goods and services.

In an article published in 2008 by the Instituto Boliviano de Comercio Exterior, the author estimates that over one million Bolivians have emigrated from Bolivia since 2000, and more than 2.5 million—over one-fourth of Bolivia's entire population—were living abroad (most moved to Argentina, Spain, the United States, and Brazil), trying to make a living they could not manage in their own country. Once Bolivians are able to get established on a job abroad, they often send 'remesas,' (a check with a portion of their earnings) back home. It is estimated that in 2006, for example, the remesas added up to about $972 million, the second most important source of income for Bolivia after natural gas. For those who have stayed behind, forty per cent are employed in agriculture, 17 per cent in industry, and 43 per cent in services (2006 est.).

In recent years, the Bolivian economy, like that of so many in the world, has had its ups and downs: an economic crisis early in the 1980s was followed by reforms and private investment in the 1990s. Again, in 2003-2005, there was more political instability, precipitated by the government's intention of exporting newly discovered natural gas reserves. In 2005, the government imposed a hydrocarbons law that assured greater profits and security for the incipient Bolivian industry. Since then, the world market for hydrocarbons has fluctuated wildly, directly impacting a Bolivian economy heavily reliant on this sole commodity for financial stability. Nevertheless, 2010 saw the biggest trade surplus in Bolivia's history, due to an increase in world commodity prices.

One final bright note in Bolivia's future economy: with the rush in the world automobile industry to mass produce vehicles using lithium-ion batteries, Bolivia's Salar de Uyuni is estimated to contain 50 per cent of the world's deposits of lithium. Already used in laptop computers and cell phones, lithium carbonate's value (and price) will rise significantly once mass production of electric cars takes hold. A United States Geological Survey estimates that 5.4 million tons of lithium could potentially be extracted from the Salar, enough to supply the automotive industry for decades.

HISTORY / POLITICS

With new archeological findings pouring in every year, Bolivia's early history has continued to be pushed back by thousands of years. Some research suggests that the Andean region has been inhabited for almost 21,000 years. More concretely, there is abundant evidence in the Bolivian altiplano to date the beginnings of the Tiahuanacotas' culture to before the Christian era. Near the shore of Lake Titicaca, Tiahuanaco became an important trade and religious center for a sophisticated culture—with advanced techniques in architecture and agriculture— that expanded greatly, until its demise around 1200 A.D. Other indigenous civilizations—the Mollos and the Moxos—inhabited other areas and disappeared about the same time as the Tiahuanacotas.

The rise of the Aymara civilization coincided with the fall of the neighboring Tiahuanacotas. They were warriors, but also advanced in irrigation, engineering, freeze-drying of food, and expansion of food production by farming the eastern lowlands of Bolivia. The Incas entered the altiplano about 1450 A.D., and brought with them the achievements of one of the most advanced civilizations in the world at that time: a highly organized culture, sophisticated knowledge in many areas, an impressive array of physical infrastructure, and a strong central government. The Aymara kingdoms became subjects of the Incas and were subjected to Incan rules and tributes, but were permitted to live autonomously.

As empires go, and in spite of all of their impressive accomplishments, the Incas didn't last that long. A civil war of succession, followed by the fall of the capital Cusco in 1534 to Spanish conquistadors and Indian allies all weakened any hope of defending the empire. But infectious diseases brought by Europeans were the greatest single determinant in the decimation of vast numbers of an empire that in its prime some experts estimate at between 15-17 million.

After the subjugation of the Incan empire, the Spanish colonization of Bolivia—under the Viceroyalty of Alto Peru— quickly took shape, following a pattern of exploitation established in the rest of their conquests in the new world. But Bolivia offered something few other places in the world could provide: a seemingly endless supply of silver. The exploitation of this precious metal and the abundance of slave labor in mines, agriculture, and construction made Spain a prosperous and powerful empire for hundreds of years. Cerro Rico (Rich Mountain), located in Potosí—the world's highest city and at the time the largest city in the Western Hemisphere—was a virtual mountain of silver. Cerro Rico was the most productive silver mine ever, mined for silver until its near depletion in 1800, and later mined mostly for tin (and some silver) well beyond the colonial period until 1984. But the dark side of all the material wealth extracted revealed that some estimated eight million Africans and indigenous workers died—including many child laborers—in abysmal abuse, subhuman working conditions, and disease during the colonial period (1545-1825).

Another major component of Spanish rule was the proselytization of the Indian population to the Catholic faith. As in every other colony in Spanish America, Jesuit missions were constructed in urban and rural areas to convert souls, but also to teach European skills in textiles, masonry, music, painting, and other useful trades. Formal education of Indians was not widespread or encouraged. Living under colonial rule, Indians were forced to accept conversion along with forced labor, payment of tributes, and restrictions on all human freedoms. Reactions to the new religion varied: some Indians adapted, many only did so superficially by clinging to local beliefs and customs and, and others totally rejected both Christianity and Spanish rule, leading to over one hundred local revolts in Bolivia and Peru.

By the late 1700s, discontent grew in the Spanish colonies among 'criollos,' (children of 'pure' Spanish descent born in the New World) who took on increasingly active roles in the economy and bureaucracy of Bolivia. Inspired by Enlightenment thought and by the American and French Revolutions, Bolivian criollos started their own independence movement from Spain in 1808. The ensuing war carried on for years, before the independence forces declared an independent republic in 1824, and named 'Bolivia' after Venezuelan liberator Simón Bolívar.

During the fledgling years of the new republic, Bolivian history was marked by the presidency of Andrés de Santa Cruz (1829-1839), who instituted many badly needed reforms in government; the War of the Confederation (1836-39); a sixty-year period of political chaos characterized by coups and short-lived constitutions; the War of the Pacific (1879-83) in which Bolivia lost to Chile territorial access to the Pacific Ocean, as well as to rich nitrate fields.

The Chaco War (1932-1935) was instigated when Bolivia sought disputed territory in the remote Chaco region (including access to the Paraguay River) controlled by Paraguay. Since losing its Pacific coastline, Bolivia needed access to the Atlantic Ocean via the Paraguay River. Bolivia lost the war, but was conceded access to the river by the terms of the armistice. The war resulted in enormous numbers of casualties for both countries, but Bolivia retained what was later discovered to be significant petroleum deposits in the eastern part of the country. Standard Oil came in to extract the crude, and eventually the holdings of Standard Oil were nationalized in 1936.

In the meantime, Bolivian politics and government, just like virtually everywhere in Latin America, were in turmoil for most of the twentieth century, with frequent coups, counter-coups, revolts, popular uprisings, military interventions, nullification of elections, makeshift coalitions, and the traditional ideological polar opposition between the haves and the have-nots.

Under Presidents Víctor Paz Estenssoro (1952-1956; 1960-64), and Hernán Siles Zuaso (1956-60) the Nationalist Revolutionary Movement Revolution put into action sweeping reforms, including universal voting rights, incorporation of the indigenous peasants into national life, land reform, rural education, and nationalization of Bolivia's largest tin mines. However, many of these reforms foundered due to lack of capital, limited resources, and insufficient administration. Land reform, for example, was only partly successful, leaving millions of peasants in oblivion, with the chronic shortage of food that had characterized Bolivia for so long. Other problems emerged: the extreme devaluation of the national currency; tin mines were largely depleted, leading to massive layoffs; food shortages were getting worse; and even massive foreign aid was not enough to alleviate these problems.

In 1964, a military coup d'état was carried out by Paz Estenssoro's own vice-president, René Barrientos and army commander Alfredo Ovando; together they ruled as co-presidents until Barrientos was officially elected president in 1966. During his term, revolutionary leader Ché Guevara was captured and killed; several massacres of hundreds of miners and their families were carried out; exiles were imposed on union leaders; and other repressive measures characterized his rule as a brutal dictatorship. Following Barrientos' death in a helicopter crash in 1969, there ensued more military coups and counter-coups, as well as short-lived, ineffectual and sometimes corrupt military juntas, and massive demonstrations.

Finally, in 1982 after a long hiatus, democracy and two ex-presidents returned to office: Hernán Siles Suazo (1982-85) and Paz Estenssoro (1985-1989). The national problems by this time were even worse than usual: social unrest, economic instability, human rights violations, and a staggering hyperinflation of 24,000 per cent, and a world collapse of tin prices, leading to massive layoffs in Bolivian mines. Jaime Paz Zamora became president in 1989, and continued much of the program of his predecessors to control inflation, terrorism, and drug trafficking, but was reluctant to prohibit coca plantations. In 1989, Gonzalo Sánchez de Lozada gained the presidency and subsequently instituted a program of a 50 per cent privatization of state-owned enterprises, including the prosperous Yacimientos Petrolíferos Fiscales Bolivianos oil corporation. General Hugo Banzer, elected in 1997, felt compelled to declare martial law in 2000 to quell massive public and civic protests against the privatization law, and later had the law repealed. Banzer later resigned in 2001 for health reasons.

After being defeated in the presidential election of 2002, Juan Evo Morales Ayva, a former 'cocalero' (coca grower) running on a coalition ticket of indigenous and social movements, ran again in 2005 and won comfortably. He thus became the first indigenous president of Bolivia, and his platform called for a re-nationalization of the natural gas industry in Bolivia, a pledge that he carried out in May, 2006. Some of his other actions were more controversial: dismissing magistrates of the Constitutional Tribunal who voted against his court-packing of the Supreme Court. He nullified the results of four referendums in eastern departments of the country that called for autonomy from the central government. And in 2007, he proposed a new constitution, which was subsequently passed in 2009, ceding to indigenous Bolivians greater economic and political rights. Beyond his program of social reform, he has gained renown for his defense of the right of Bolivia to cultivate coca, and for his rejection of traditional United States pressure on determining Bolivian governance.

Morales social program has aimed at diminishing extreme poverty and illiteracy among the indigenous population. He introduced old-age pensions, natal and pediatric clinics, price controls for gasoline and foodstuffs, incentives for home-grown produce, and inflation controlling measures. He won a second term in office in 2009 by a landslide, and his Movement for Socialism party won a two-thirds majority in both chambers of the legislature.

SOCIETY

Notwithstanding social and economic reforms in the past half century in Bolivia, it continues to be beset by crushing poverty and insufficient infrastructure, land, and resources to address persistent social problems. In addition to the enormous migration of Bolivians to other countries in search of a better life, the internal migration to cities from rural areas—where subsistence farming has been a perennial struggle—has not helped increase agricultural production, nor diminished the problems of accelerated urbanization. Added to that are the tens of thousands of unemployed indigenous miners and their families who continue to gravitate to El Alto—just outside of La Paz—a megalopolis of close to a million inhabitants, described by some as the "capital of social protest in Bolivia".

The majority of Bolivians are indigenous: Quechua 30% and Aymara 25%; followed by mestizo (mixed white and Amerindian ancestry) 30%; and white 15%. Official figures show that the predominant religion in Bolivia—as in all of Latin America—is Roman Catholic (95%), and Protestant (5%); numbers that clearly do not include all of Bolivian society. The socio-economic status of the ethnic groups closely coincides with distinct racial divisions established almost 500 years ago: the wealthiest are invariably those lighter-skinned descendants of European stock; next follows the bi-racial mestizos, and at the bottom of the scale is the impoverished indigenous sector.

For education, 2009 figures from UNESCO show that 90.7 per cent of adults and 99.1 per cent of youth (15 years and older) are literate. Compulsory schooling is through grade eight, but almost 25 per cent of children do not attend school. Secondary school attendance is lower; about 44 per cent of age-appropriate children do not attend school. Attendance rates for primary and secondary schools are much higher in urban areas. There are forty-eight universities in Bolivia. Only about 5 per cent of secondary school graduates go on to universities, and of those only about one per cent receives a university degree.

BIBLIOGRAPHY

http://www.boliviabella.com/history.html
http://www.census.gov/population/international
     /files/ib-9801.pdf
https://www.cia.gov/library/publications/the-world-
     factbook/geos/bl.html
http://www.citypopulation.de/Bolivia.html
Cockcroft, James D. *Latin America: History, Politics,
     and U.S. Policy*. 2nd ed. Chicago: Nelson-Hall, 1995.
http://devdata.worldbank.org/AAG/bol_aag.pdf
Goodwin, Paul B. *Latin America*. 14th ed. Dubuque, Iowa:
     McGraw-Hill/ 2010, 2010.
Herring, Hubert. *A History of Latin America*. New York:
     Alfred A. Knopf, 1963.
http://huebler.blogspot.com/2006/05/secondary-school
     -attendance-in-bolivia.html
http://www.ibce.org.bo/ComExt/comext159.pdf
http://www.indexmundi.com/bolivia/
http://www.infoplease.com/ipa/A0001771.html
http://www.infoplease.com/ce6/world/A0856956.html
http://www.nytimes.com/2009/02/03/world/americas/
     03lithium.html?pagewanted=all
http://stats.uis.unesco.org/unesco/TableViewer/
     document.aspx?ReportId=121&IF_Language=eng&BR
     _Country=680&BR_Region=40520
http://es.wikipedia.org/wiki/Geograf%C3%ADa_de_Bolivia
The World Factbook: https://www.cia.gov/library/publications/the-
world-factbook/

Andean Journeys:
A Bilingual Anthology of
Contemporary Bolivian Poetry

1

Jorge Campero

2

A BOCA DE JARRO

La risa helada hasta los críos
mi ojo es una cerradura con llave
es la noche del saltimbanqui festivo
los cerdos comen flores para reponerse
el signo del zodíaco
no dice nada de la fecha en que muerdo
desolaciones
pesada la tricolor bandera
ella de boca abierta para el bostezo
la nación
es como una niña que se juega en celo al amor
es la voz de mi quemadura + vidrios
que adentro testifican
la pared está descascarada
asoman pajas y ánimas
escondo dentro de mí
a los que gritan de esquina a esquina
de la Av. Buenos Aires en noviembre
arrastro un pie cojo en el recuerdo
y bajo la sombra de mi lengua
                        espero.
No será una fruta.

A boca de jarro

****

POEMA DE UN MALIENTE

Si no regreso. . .
La noche abre la puerta
y la fatalidad
cae
en el extraño nombre del día
en un puñal
"diles. . . que los quero mucho"
Una enorme rosa roja
ha florecido en mi caja toráxica
del tamaño de una oreja
a la otra
y estoy llorando a borbotones
por la enorme rosa roja
"Mi viejita" mi ansiedad
oscura

AT POINT BLANK

Frozen laughter even for newborns
my eye is a lock with a key
it's the night of the festive acrobat
pigs eat flowers to get over it
the zodiac sign
is mute about the date when I'll bite on
desolation
the tri-color flag is sluggish
she is open-mouthed for a yawn
the nation
is like a girl who stakes her fervor on love
it's the voice of my burnt skin + window glass
that testify inside me
the wall is peeling
pieces of straw and purgatory souls appear
within me I hide
those who shout from corner to corner
on Buenos Aires Avenue in November
I drag along my lame foot in the memory
and I lower the shadow of my tongue

I wait.

It probably isn't a fruit.

A boca de jarro

****

POEM OF A TROUBLEMAKER

If I don't return…
Night will open the door
and misfortune
will fall
on the strange name of day
on a dagger
"tell them …that I love them very much"
An enormous red rose
has blossomed on my thoracic cavity
with a size from one ear
to the other
and I am crying furiously
because of this enormous red rose
"My little old lady" my dark
anxiety

amarras de alambre el respiro que hace ruido
cruza el patio
camina sobre la madera seca
la noche cierra la puerta
hija de la tarde
miel de abeja tu corazón

Svmarivm Comvn sobre vivos

****

EL TEQUILA DEL MARIACHI
A Carlos Rivera

Me sabe a pólvora que se llevó uno vivo
A perro mudo envenenado huelo
Rezo por redimirme de este purgatorio
Agua viva que rasguñas
El animita se santigua
—paisaje con guajolotes y caballo muerto—
Me encielo pero me abajaron
Dicen que dicen que los amores de cantina
no duran ni el luto reglamentario
—me lo dijo un matrero—
Amigo
aguántame este berrinche
siquiera un tantito
Hazme un pie de gato
La resaca hace su trabajo
Aún la llevo conmigo
como una 30-30 en bandolera.

El corazón ardiente

****

MUSA EN JEANS DESCOLORIDO

En el mesón los interminables platos de ajíes tamales y
humitas para dos calaveras / donde hacemos titánicas
pulsetas / por olvidar ese pedazo de película / cuando Ud.
era una medalla de mi charretera / o la brisa de mi caballo
/ mi bandera de guerra / entonces los dos acostados sobre
el mapamundi / al calor de las refriegas / las noches / la
música de los zancudos / esperándonos con los brazos en
jarra / cerca al hito de la frontera / se nos enfundaba la

you wire up the breath that makes noise
cross the patio
walk upon the dry wood
night closes the door
daughter of the afternoon
your heart is bees' honey.

Svmarivm Comvn sobre vivos

****

THE MARIACHI'S TEQUILA
For Carlos Rivera

To me it tastes like gunpowder someone ran off with
I smell like a mute, poisoned dog
I pray to redeem myself from this purgatory
Running water that you scratch
The little soul makes the sign of the cross
—a landscape with turkeys and a dead horse—
I get jealous but they calm me down
There's a saying that cantina romances
don't last even long enough for the official mourning
—a shrewd guy once told me—
Friend,
be patient with this tantrum
just a little bit
Make me a cat's paw
The hangover does its work
I still carry it around
like a 30-30 in a bandoleer.

El corazón ardiente

****

MUSE IN FADED JEANS

In the inn the interminable dishes of chilies, tamales and
sweet tamales for two skeletons / where we do titanic
hand-wrestling / to forget that bit of a movie / when you
were a medal on my epaulette / or the breeze of my horse
/ my war pennant / then the two of us lying on the
map of the world / under the heat of the skirmishes / the nights /
the music of the mosquitos / waiting for us with their arms in
a pitcher / near the boundary stone of the border / our desire to

gana de jugar a la taba en los días de lluvia marcados en el
Bristol claveteado en la pared / sabiendo lo tarde que es
para esperar el tren que viene del sur / otra resaca que triza
el alma / y los kilos de los años son el plomo de los
fusilamientos / pues / le diré / que conocerla no fue en
vano / y como último favor / quiero haga una visera con
sus manos / para observar los gallinazos revoltear los
círculos de mi victoria / cuando descienden por mi carroña
/ a los campos de batalla donde sembramos lechugas / por
favor no los espante.

*   *   *   *   *

NO APTA PARA MENORES

Noche bajo la lluvia
Seborrea de ángeles
Confabulando el silencio de las máquinas industriales
Borrachos con misereres en las tabernas
Acompañados de calurosas de pelo recogido
Con un tic tac automático entre los senos
Una presea sagrada
Maquillaje de primer debut
Pérfida caminando por el alambre
De ida al matadero
Poblada por pesadillas y un amor de película
Enciendes un cigarrillo y lees la inicial del que te recuerda
Exhalas una aureola de santo
Cruzas las piernas electrocutando el sexo oral de los poetas
Alguien enchufado en corriente trifásica
Pelando los dientes
Adorado sukiyaki en la gran sartén del mundo
Platillo favorito de un mátalas-callando-cójelas-al-vuelo
Alargada pantera platinada en el écran
Con un ramo de cartuchos.
Manzana prohibida en otra mesa
Manzana del prójimo en un film de la vida real
Y el adiós de voz aflautada de los crueles-crueles
El rouge mortal de las típicas tiñendo las despedidas
Y los anturios
Ambos buscando la lagartija del amor
En el gran patio del mundo
Con la viviente cola entre los dedos
No conduce con las estrellas y astros
Irse a pie taconeando los kilómetros que faltan
Dejando atrás ciudades enterradas

play knucklebones was muffled on the rainy days marked
on the Bristol board nailed on the wall / knowing how late
it is to await the train coming from the south / another hangover
that shreds the soul / and the kilos of the years are the lead of
the shootings / well/ I'll tell you / that meeting her was not in
vain /and as a last favor / I want you to make a shade with your
hands/ to observe the chicken hawks circle over the circles
of my victory / when they descend for my carcass /on the
battlefields where we planted lettuce / please don't
scare them away.

*   *   *   *   *

NOT FIT FOR MINORS

Night under rain
Seborrhea of angels
Conspiring the silence of industrial machines
Drunks with misereres in taverns
Accompanied by hot chicks with pinned-up hair
With automatic tick tocks between their breasts
A sacred jewel
Makeup in its debut
The perfidious one walking on the wire
On the way to the slaughterhouse
Beset by nightmares and a love like in the movies
You light a cigarette and read the initial of one who remembers you
You exhale a halo of a saint
You cross your legs executing the oral sex of poets
Someone plugged into three-phased electric current
Baring his teeth
Adored sukiyaki in the great frying pan of the world
A favorite dish of a kill-them-quietly-grab-them-in-flight
An elongated, silver-plated panther on the screen
With a cluster of cartridges.
A forbidden apple on another table
The neighbor's apple in a film of real life
And the goodbye in the reedy voice of the cruel-cruel
The mortal rouge of the typical ones tinting their goodbyes
And the flamingo flowers
Both searching for the lizard of love
In the great patio of the world
With their lively tail between their fingers
It doesn't behave with the stars and the heavenly bodies
Leaving on foot, strutting through the kilometers ahead
Leaving behind buried cities

8

Bajo una lluvia cósmica
Entre la lejanía y las mandíbulas del cielo y la tierra
Así inscritos en los créditos
El que se enoja pierde
Después del rugido del león de la Metro Goldwyn Mayer
Empieza nuestra película de jinetes celestiales
Doblada al español.

* * * * *

ANIMAL URBANO

Lenguas negras de las autopistas de alta velocidad / te
llevarán a las ciudades del desamor / hambreadas que la
ilusión pinta en las fachadas / sólo carcajadas dolorosas /
colmenares con ventanas al sol que son bocas / aguas de
color y luces y publicidad con antiguos rostros que ríen /
rostros de los idos / vestidos de espejuelos y baratijas /
perfumadas tristezas / piedras del sacrificio / ciudades de
piedras falsas / casas de empeño / capitales fornicias de
jugosas frutas casi humanas / con alma de billete / cuerpos
que se quiebran o se venden / recitadores de palabras a la
vez que cazan una mosca / sórdidas habitaciones y paredes
con anónimos que se quejan / industriales salones para
seleccionar carne / "la fuerza eléctrica, la fuerza mecánica o
una hostia el menú del día" / entonan los ejércitos de
estacionados / flores de plástico en los basurales / lloran
los ojos de agua que la tierra puso para su vigilancia / por
las noches en el cuadrante o tesado tambor / se escucha
aullar lejanos domésticos / es por ti / cantores tristes de
pueblos remotos adormecen el sueño / es por ti.

* * * * *

HOTEL PIJUAN

En este lugar te vi llover
Niebla nupcial en el cerro Uchumachi*
Parada de los dioses que escribieron sus nombres
En las paredes
Modesta la habitación
Encerrados en un cubo
Temo te espanten las manchas en el tumbado
Tarántulas de dieciséis rubíes
Nos quitamos la cáscara
El amor siempre será impuro

Under a cosmic rain
Between remoteness and the mandibles of heaven and earth
So inscribed in the credits
He who gets angry loses
After the roar of the lion of Metro Goldwyn Mayer
Our movie of celestial horsemen begins
Dubbed in Spanish

*   *   *   *   *

URBAN ANIMAL

Black tongues of high-speed highways / will take you to
cities of indifference / famished that illusion paints on the
façades / only painful guffaws / beehives with windows
facing the sun like mouths / colored water and lights and
publicity with aged faces that laugh / faces of loonies /
dressed up in glitter and cheap jewelry / perfumed sadness /
sacrificial stones; cities of false stones / pawn shops /
fornicating capitals of juicy fruits almost human / with a
soul of cash / bodies that break down or are for sale /
reciters of words who hunt flies at the same time / sordid
rooms and walls with anonymous graffiti of complaints /
industrial rooms set up to select meat / "electrical power,
mechanical power or a Eucharistic wafer on today's menu" /
armies of parked vehicles tune their horns / plastic flowers
in garbage cans / eyes sprout tears from the water earth
provided for its vigilance / for the nights in the cuadrant or
the testate drum / you can hear the howling of distant servants /
it's on account of you /sad singers from remote towns become
drowsy and sleep / on account of you.

*   *   *   *   *

HOTEL PIJUAN

In this place I saw you rain
A nuptial fog on the Uchumachi hill*
A parade of gods who wrote their names
On the walls
A modest room
Enclosed in a cubicle
I fear the stains on the ceiling will scare you
Tarantulas of sixteen rubies
We remove the shell
Love will always be impure

Venidos a luchar como inmortales
Hasta pechos de bronce sangran
En ocasiones parecidas.

* Uchumachi: al lado de Coroico, a 95 kms. de La Paz

*   *   *   *   *

RETRATO DE VACA SAGRADA

Adorable masca un adams
Verde planicie pastos verdes
Bajo quitasoles de palmeras

Cantando muuuu

Enamorada mira la aguada
El cuadro enmarcado
Con alambres de púas
Postes semienterrados
Una bandada de endomingados
Karcanchos zopilotes suchas
O buitres esperan ir con el cuento
Que las vacas sagradas
Mañana serán albóndigas.

*   *   *   *   *

EL SIN BOLERO

Hombrecito oscuro marengo
Escondido entrepapelado
En cuentos contables
Eructando hambre
En el escalafón de los tribunos
Se fue un día de fútbol
A mirar el team de sus amores
Un día de muchos goles
Entre festejo y festejo
Y chin chin de copas
En el bar desenrolló su lengua
Una arenga y se ganó
La expulsión del paraíso
Sin traje
Sin trabajo
sin bolero

We've come to battle like immortals
Even bronze breasts can bleed
On similar occasions.

*Urumachi hill: next to Coroico, 60 miles from La Paz

*   *   *   *   *

PORTRAIT OF SACRED COW

It's adorable as it chews on a Chiclet
A green plain, green grasses
Below palm-tree parasols

Singing moooo

Enamored, it observes the watering hole
The picture is framed
With barbed wire
Partially sunken posts
A flock of Patagonian monsters, buzzards,
Suchas, or vultures dressed in their Sunday best
All hoping to tell the story
That the sacred cows
Tomorrow will be meat balls.

*   *   *   *   *

MAN WITHOUT BOLERO

Little man dark, grayish
Hidden, half-papered
In bookkeeper accounts
Burping up hunger
On the promotion list of the tribunes
He left on a football day
To watch his beloved team
A day of many goals
Between celebrations and rejoicings
Between the cheers and cheers of drinks
In the bar his tongue unwound
A harangue and he earned
An expulsion from paradise
Without a suit
Without work
Without a bolero

Sin Eva
Sin boleto
Sin sin
Sin team
Sin billetes
Con etcéteras
Escribiendo poemas
Desde Actarius
Lugar de su última residencia.

Musa en jeans descolorido

*   *   *   *

JAGUAR AZUL

Una señal del dios Uks
Arañas peludas de ónix extendieron trampas
En la oración con molares y garganta oscura
Te quisiera de nuevo conmigo para corretear al atardecer
Que escucharas la música de agua que has abandonado
El silencio de nuestras huellas
Hormigas presurosas sin nadita de sueño
Recorriendo los árboles
—Falos de la tierra—
La sangrienta caoba y una montaña
Tarde mismamente no llega el sol
Y se necesitan camas de hojas
A la sombra tu carne se olisca
Viajando en círculos las canciones de las moscas verdes
Sobre su costillar orificios de plomo olor a pólvora
Alimentada de frutos silvestres
Ríos con peces y constelaciones
Y la sola tonada del monte naruru naruruuu
De rato en rato la oración fúnebre de las parabas
En la espesura viento y ramas continúan la última tormenta
Rememoro esa sangrante senda
Como eras todo
Lamí la pedrería para recogerte

El tiempo enseña que todo es agua

A cada tarde
Si la riada te devuelve...
Escarbando no te puedo encontrar
Tras la mirada del jaguar

Without Eve
Without a ticket
Without a without
Without a team
Without tickets
With etceteras
Writing poems
From Actarius
The place of his last residence.

Musa de jeans descolorido

*　　　　*　　　　*　　　　*　　　　*

BLUE JAGUAR

A sign from the god Uks
Hairy onyx spiders laid out their traps
In the prayer with molars and a dark throat
I'd like you to be here with me again to pursue the dusk
So you could hear the water's music you've abandoned
The silence of our footprints
Ants scurrying about, not at all sleepy
Passing by the trees
—Phalluses of the land—
The bloody mahogany and the mountain
The sun doesn't exactly come out late
And beds of leaves are needed
In the shade your flesh smells intensely
The songs of the green flies circling around
On her ribs orifices of lead, smell of gunpowder
Fed on wild fruit
Rivers with fish and constellations
And the only melody of the forest naruru naruruu
From time to time the funeral prayer of the macaws
In the thicket, wind and branches prolong the last storm
I recall that bloody path
Everything about you
I licked the precious stones to retrieve you

Time teaches that everything is water

Every afternoon
If the flood brings you back…
And by digging I can't find you
In search of the jaguar's gaze

En medio a medio
El alto sol en la loma
La brisa la oración de la tarde somos tu sepultura
Plata que la noche empolla
Y el monte no me pide te olvide del todo
Tengo que enterrarte bajo una piedra
Sembrarte para que luego vuelvas
Jaguar azul

*   *   *   *   *

LA MATANZA DE MURUCUYATI[1]

En el llorar del viento
           vuelven los guerreros
Montados a pelo
           en caballos sangrientos
Los ojos vueltos persiguiendo
           las huellas de las incursiones
Corajudos por la bronca
           mieles y guarapo[2] y chicha[3]
Delante la mordedura del fuego
Beben danzan cantan lloran braman
En el griterío llaman a sus muertos
Murucuyati es un coágulo
Otra mancha en la historia
Trapiche de la amargura
Murucuyati espeso escupitajo
Un juramento Aguará[4] un juramento
De los cabellos largos
Cabellos del viento
Emboscada de los guerreros invisibles
Para chuzar el disco del sol rojo
Las cuñas agarran los dolores verdaderos de las guerras
Como siempre serán las vencidas
Cargadas de sus cachorros de teta
Las piezas de las matanzas.

---

[1] Murucuyati: Lugar de la matanza de chiriguanos por
    mestizos y blancos avecindados en el río Azero en 1877.
[2] Guarapo: Bebida fermentada.
[3] Trapiche: Molienda de caña
[4] Aguará: Zorro, padre del primer hombre.

Jaguar Azul

****

Plumb in the middle
The high sun on the hill
We—the breeze, the afternoon prayer—are your tomb
Silver that night hatches
The forest doesn't ask me to just forget you
I have to bury you under a rock
To plant you so that you will return
Blue jaguar

*   *   *   *   *

THE MASSACRE AT MURUCUYATI[1]

In the weeping of the wind
                    the warriors return
Mounted bareback
                    on bloody horses
With eyes directed, pursuing
                    the tracks of the incursions
Enflamed by the skirmish
                    honey and guarapo[2] and chicha[3]
Before the bite of the fire
They drink dance sing cry bellow
In all the clamor they call to their fallen
Murucuyati is a clot
Another stain in history
A mill of bitterness
Murucuyati, a thick spittle
An oath, Aguará[4], an oath
Of long hair
Hair of the wind
An ambush of the invisible warriors
To wound the disk of the red sun
Wedges grab the real sorrows of wars
Just as the vanquished will always be
Burdened with newborn pups
The pieces of massacres.

---

[1]Murucuyati: Site of a massacre of the chiriguano tribe
        by neighboring mestizos and Europeans in 1877
[2] Guarapo: a fermented beverage
[3] Trapiche: a sugar-cane mill
[4] Aguará: Zorro, father of the first man.

Jaguar azul

****

2

Benjamín Chávez

COMO UN NÚMERO CUALQUIERA

Cruzar
por ciertos ya viejos lugares
vestido de manera que combine con el clima
y con unos zapatos color rutina.
O comer todos los días
cualquier cosa sobre la hora.
Buscar vacíos por donde colarse,
derramar cansancio como un pedazo de papel
en el asfalto. . .

A veces las trastadas las
protagonizan los trastes sucios,
no sólo las gentes y
las condiciones adversas.

Mientras se redime la palabra
los actos aguijonean las sienes.
¿Qué más que detenerse en la acera
sintiéndote uno
entre millones de incógnitos intentando
desencapucharse en silencio,
con perfume a chimeneas desalmadas
cargando insomnes una soga en el cuello?

¡Calla!
Tus gesticulaciones
son vulgares y para el olvido.
Es mejor visto por todos,
Guardar silencio y cumplir
un miserable rol
protagonizando los estertores.

Prehistorias del androide

*   *   *   *

FLASH

Hay una pared en lo profundo
Donde la luz se despedaza
Digno fondo para retratos metálicos
Que beberán en silencio
Del bebedero astral
De gardenias enfiladas al abismo.

LIKE ANY OTHER NUMBER

Crossing
through certain old places
dressed by matching clothes
and routine-colored shoes for the weather.
Or eating every day
anything at all, right on every hour.
Searching to squeeze into some empty space
to spill fatigue like a scrap of paper
on the asphalt.

Sometimes dirty tricks
are played out by dirty dishes,
not just by people
and adverse conditions.

While the word is liberated,
actions sting one's temples.
What's left besides stopping on a sidewalk
feeling like you're just one
among millions in incognito trying
to lower their hoods in silence,
with a perfume of merciless chimneys
sleeplessly lugging a rope around their necks?

Quiet!
Your gesticulations
are vulgar and forgettable.
It will appear better to everyone,
To keep silent and to carry out
a miserable role
playing the lead role in death rattles.

Prehistorias del androide

*   *   *   *

FLASH

There's a wall in the depths
Where light breaks into pieces
A good backdrop for metallic portraits
That will drink in silence
From the astral watering trough
Of gardenias lined up at the abysm.

En otro tiempo
La pared en lo profundo
Habría servido para deslumbrar.
Ahora soporta, creo
El desgarro
La impiedad
El peso insospechado
De toda la desmesura de la noche.
El vertiginoso paso de los días
La derrumba lentamente
Escrupulosamente.
En otro tiempo
Este poema
Habría podido llamarse
Relámpago de magnesio.

Santo sin devoción

*   *   *   *

Con manos salvadoras
abres un cajón de medicinas
—ademanes curativos de enfermera piadosa—
y sigo enumerando
la aromática fragancia de tus muñecas
los débiles tallos de tus dedos.
Habrás de verme
persistente
como un coleóptero
tras el aceite de tu lámpara
en el ritual de la apertura
porque en tu palma
trazan la ruta
las líneas de la vida
y quiero en ellas
leer mi destino.
Este es el principio
de un naufragio de proporciones orgiásticas.

*   *   *   *

Con minuciosidad de boticario
recorro todos los carteles
los frascos de vidrio
las confiterías, las tiendas
y en el fondo de un bar deshidratado

In another time
The wall in the depths
Might have served to be dazzling.
Now it supports, I believe,
Brazenness
Impiety
The unexpected weight
Of all the excesses of night.
The dizzying passage of the days
Demolishes it slowly
Scrupulously.
In another time,
This poem
Could have been called
Lightening of magnesium.

Santo sin devoción

*   *   *   *

With saving hands
you open a medicine drawer
—the curative manners of a pious nurse—
and I go on enumerating
the aromatic fragrance of your wrists
the weak stems of your fingers.
You probably perceive me
as persistent
like a coleopteran beetle
attracted to the oil of your lamp
in the ritual of an opening
because in your palm
the lines of life
lay out the route
and I want to read
my destiny in them.
This is the beginning
of a shipwreck of orgiastic proportions.

*   *   *   *

With the minuteness of a druggist
I look over all the posters
the glass jars
the candy shops, the stores
and at the back of a dehydrated bar

veo mi reflejo y me siento
un gusano aferrado a los últimos vahos del mezcal.
Las ciudades son gradas mecánicas
que te alejan sin cesar.
Huyendo doblo una esquina con mi biceps de hierro
y me muerde una boca de lobo.
La luna, francotirador infalible
me ha encañonado sin remedio.
Una bala con fulguraciones e plata
hollará mi corazón
entretenida en la venganza.

Y allá en lo alto un pedazo de cielo

*   *   *   *

INAUDIBLE (25)

notas
tachaduras
anotaciones al margen
apenas eso
el aporte

*   *   *   *

INAUDIBLE (26)

palabra
inventada
como todas
como ninguna

Extramuros

*   *   *   *

MINIMAL

La quietud estalla en mis oídos
y la contemplación pavorosa
resquebraja los objetos.
Fragmento tumultuoso en
torbellino quieto,
el mundo penetra desbordado
y astilla las líneas

I see my reflection and I feel like
a worm clinging to the last fumes of the mescal.
Cities are escalating steps
that ceaselessly take you away.
Fleeing, I turn a corner with my iron biceps
and I'm bitten by danger.
The moon, an infallible sharpshooter,
has unavoidably aimed at me.
A bullet with flashes and silver
will trample on my heart,
entertained in vengeance.

Y allá en lo alto un pedazo de cielo

*   *   *   *

INAUDIBLE (25)

notes
erasures
notes in the margin
hardly that
the contribution

*   *   *   *

INAUDIBLE (26)

word
invented
like all of them
like none

Extramuros

*   *   *   *

MINIMAL

The quiet breaks out in my ears
and its terrified contemplation
cracks objects.
A tumultuous fragment in a
quiet whirlwind,
the world, overflowed, penetrates
and splinters the lines

24

de todas las ficciones.
Recomponerlas—tarea que tienta.
Lubricar los moldes
calzar las voces
obrar como dioses
con instrumentos de lata
y alma de perejil.

*   *   *   *

RITUAL

Viendo fotografías de inmensas ciudades
para mí totalmente irreales
me fuiste señalando
con la guía del índice
el profundo pasado de tu ventura.
Toda la noche recorrimos tus recuerdos
de siete mares y otras tantas vidas
hasta recalar
¿por fin?
en mi puerto.

*   *   *   *

LA DÉBIL MÚSICA DE LAS SUAVES COSAS

En la alta noche
la débil música de las suaves cosas.
Mientras el sueño consuma la quietud
las torres callan
los motivos de tu altura.
Cada instante se estremece
y lo quedo nos habla con una voz más íntima.
No son las cosas que no tendremos nunca
son las que están
las que estuvieron siempre
y hoy
—complicidad contenida—
nos susurran
una familiaridad irresuelta.

*   *   *   *

of all the fictions.
To fix them again—a tempting task.
Oiling the molds
wedging the voices
laboring like gods
with tin instruments
and a soul of parsley.

*   *   *   *

RITUAL

Seeing photos of immense cities
totally unreal for me
you went on pointing
with the guidance of your index finger
the deep past of your luck.
All night long we reviewed your memories
of seven seas and as many other lives
until your ship reaches land
at last?
in my port.

*   *   *   *

THE WEAK MUSIC OF SOFT THINGS

Late at night
the weak music of soft things.
While sleep consumes the stillness
the towers conceal
the motives of your pitch.
Every instant trembles
and the stillness speaks to us with a more intimate voice.
They are not things that we will never have,
they are things that are here
things that always were
and today
—a contained complicity—
they whisper to us
an unresolved familiarity.

*   *   *   *

RELACIÓN NOMINAL DE BAJAS

Mesas vacías.
La barra atiborrada de vasos exhaustos.
Cubos de agua con detergente
balbuceando protestas trasnochadas.
Sillas durmiendo la mona
—cansado campamento de refugiados—.
El frío por las rendijas de la puerta.
Solitario el barman
con su solitario café y rubios infinitos
medita,
compasivo
las exaltadas vidas,
las derrochadas muertes
de la noche que acaba.
Sin novedad, concluye
—desmantelado altar de los desvelos—
la rutina del bar
a las seis de la mañana.

Pequeña librería de viejo

****

NOMINAL LIST OF THE FALLEN

Empty tables.
The bar stacked with exhausted glasses.
Buckets of water with detergent
babbling all-night protests.
Chairs sleeping off a hangover
—a tired camp of refugees.
Cold traversing the cracks of the door.
The solitary barman
with his solitary coffee and infinite blonds
meditates,
compassionate,
the exalted lives,
the wasteful deaths
in a night that ends.
Nothing happening, he concludes
—a dismantled altar of sleeplessness—
the routine of the bar
at six in the morning.

Pequeña librería de viejo

****

3

Eduardo Mitre

DESDE TU CUERPO
(Fragmentos)

a Gabriel

Tú apenas nacido
y ya ansío que crezcas
para que hablemos,
hijo,
de niño a niño.

*   *   *

Me alejo, descubro
tu ausencia.
Te escribo el poema.
Lo ignora
tu inocencia.

*   *   *

Suplico a los dioses:
que crezca simple como la hierba
y fuerte como el roble.
O mejor que no crezca.

*   *   *

Miro tus manos que agarran
un muñeco de trapo.
Veo monedas y sangre
y tiemblo por ambos lados.

Hay un país solo, triste,
pobre, mágico, difícil,
casi imposible.
Errantes nosotros,
hijo, de allí nomás somos.

El placer de comer
no te lo quiten las penas.
Ni menos te lo conviertan
apetito de poder.

Te imagino en el alba
(despiertos los dioses)

FROM YOUR BODY
(Fragments)

to Gabriel

You've just been born
and I already wish you'd grow up
so we can talk,
son,
child to child.

*   *   *

I move away and discover
your absence.
I write you a poem.
Your innocence
is unaware of it.

*   *   *

I plead with the gods:
that he grow up easily like grass
and strong like an oak.
Better yet, that he not grow up.

*   *   *

I watch your hands that grasp
a rag doll.
I see coins and blood
and I tremble on both sides.

There is a country, lonely, sad,
poor, magical, difficult,
almost impossible.
Wandering we are,
son, we're from just over there.

Don't let sorrows take away
your pleasure of eating.
Nor worse, let them convert
it to a hunger for power.

I imagine you at daybreak
(the gods are watchful)

entre una multitud colmada de dones
limpia de dádivas.

Desde tu cuerpo

****

ROSTRO EN BLANCO

Sin fecha memorable
ni lugar preciso
íntimamente
nace el olvido.

Callado
como el cadáver de un río,
ajeno, inevitable
como el destino,

sombra espesa,
estatua terminante,
rostro disuelto en rasgos
sin sentido, nace.

Nace y una tarde
de tardío asombro,
sin júbilo ni grito,
se descubre que ha nacido.

(En cuál hora de mis horas,
en qué día de mis días
te he perdido?)

Ferviente humo

****

LA VACA

Eso en el valle a lo lejos no es una cabaña
Eso en el valle a lo lejos es la vaca
Paz forrada de viento la vaca
Agua y nieve el cielo y la vaca leche y queso
La vaca está comiendo para eso
Ajena al tiempo y a lo que pienso de la vaca
está la vaca.

*   *   *   *

among masses replete with talents
but bereft of all gifts.

Desde tu cuerpo

****

A BLANK FACE

With no memorable date
nor precise location
intimately
oblivion is born.

Quiet
like a river's corpse,
remote, inevitable
like destiny,

a thick shadow,
a conclusive statue,
a face dissolved into senseless
features, is born.

It's born and one afternoon
a belated surprise:
with no joy, no shouting,
its birth is discovered.

(In which hour of all my hours,
on which day of all my days
have I lost you?)

Ferviente humo

****

THE COW

That over there in the valley is not a cabin
That over there in the valley is the cow
Peace covered by wind is the cow
Water and snow are the sky and the cow is milk and cheese
The cow is eating for that
Beyond time and beyond what I think of the cow
is the cow.

*   *   *   *

LA SILLA

NO ECHA RAÍCES como el armario la silla que sólo
se posa como los pájaros
La silla era un ave de ala portátil y vuelo escaso (sobre
los hombros en fiesta pasaban la silla como una cigüeña)
Con viento y papeles es ya palomar
En los velorios nadie alivia más que la silla
Encapuchada con una camisa amanece la silla
Tarántula erguida en la penumbra la silla
La silla espirita junto a la mesa
Como el poema la silla es un atado de líneas
La silla sostiene al que escribe estas líneas

*   *   *   *

CONVERGENCIA

El solitario del camino discurriendo por un
bosque de lámparas doradas cruza un puente sobre
el lago donde flota un hábito de vidrio del que emerge
una doncella que danzando como Shiva lo fascina hasta
atraerlo y sumergirlo en su ardiente lecho de algas.
Noche ya más tarde en la playa de un silencio
blanco unos ojos y una mano que aún gotean trazan
letra a letra el camino del solitario.

Mirabilia

****

LA LUZ DEL REGRESO
(Fragmento)

a Gabriel

3

Con un ligero temblor
empuja
la puerta del baño.
Al fondo,
        frente a sus años,
atento
como un ciego a los pasos,
aguarda el espejo.

THE CHAIR

The chair that just reposes like birds
doesn't sink roots like a wardrobe
The chair was a portable-winged bird of short flights (at
parties the chair passed about on shoulders like a stork)
With wind and papers it's now a pigeon coop
At funerals, no one comforts more than the chair
The chair starts the day hooded with a shirt
The chair: a tarantula erect in the penumbra
The chair stirs next to the table
Like the poem, the chair is a bundle of lines
The chair supports the one who writes these lines

*   *   *   *

CONVERGENCE

The lonely one on the road roaming through a
forest of golden lamps, crosses a bridge over a
lake where a glass habit floats and from which
emerges a maiden who, dancing like Shiva
entices him and submerges him in her burning
bed of algae. Later that night on the beach of a
white silence, some eyes and a hand, still dripping,
lay out letter- by- letter the route of the lonely one.

Mirabilia

****

THE RETURNING LIGHT
   (Fragment)

to Gabriel

3

With a slight tremor
he pushes open
the bathroom door.
At the back,
        facing his years
attentive
like a blind man to footsteps,
the mirror awaits.

Se asoma
y de pronto
        como de otra
orilla del tiempo
un muchacho y un niño
lo miran sin reconocerlo.
—Piadosa la visión
sólo dura un parpadeo.

La luz del regreso

****

BELDAD

Su cabellera de Botticelli,
la corta falda negra,
sus bellísimas piernas,
sus grandes ojos verdes.

Su voz de mesa en mesa.
La blancura de su mano
volante en cada vaso
al posar la cerveza.

Sus senos que se encrespan
como las olas del mar.
Sus uñas, tajantes como la sal,
en el platillo con la cuenta.

Por ella frecuento el bar
como los fieles su iglesia.

Camino de cualquier parte

****

APARTAMENTOS

Llegan y se instalan en ellos
con la terca ilusión
de un nuevo comienzo.

Entusiastas, les quitan o añaden
muebles, cuadros,
cortinas, espejos.

He looks in
and suddenly
        as if from another
shore of time
a boy and a small child
look back without recognizing him.
—Mercifully the vision
only lasts the blink of an eye.

La luz del regreso

****

A BEAUTY

A head of hair from Boticelli
a short, black skirt,
her exquisite legs,
her huge green eyes.

Her voice from table to table.
The whiteness of her hand
flying from glass to glass
when placing down the beer.

Her breasts that roll
like waves of the sea.
Her fingernails, cutting like salt,
on the dish with the check.

It's for her that I frequent the bar
like the faithful go to church.

Camindo de cualquier parte

****

APARTMENTS

They arrive and move into them
with the obstinate illusion
of a new beginning.

All enthused, they add or subtract
furniture, pictures,
curtains, mirrors.

Los inauguran con una fiesta.
Y los habitan, haciéndose el amor
por un tiempo, y luego,
poco a poco, la guerra.

Hasta que un día,
cada uno por su cuenta,
empaca y se va,
dejándolos solos
como un escenario vacante
para los que sin duda vendrán
acaso a representar
la misma comedia.

*   *   *   *

CIUDAD A PRIMERA VISTA

Dos Ríos como dos brazos
que la ciñen y estrechan.

Puentes que cuelgan
y brillan como pulseras.

Calles que suben y bajan
lo mismo que la marea.

Barrios que a diario amanecen
al Pentecostés de las lenguas.

Parques donde la luz y la brisa
juegan a las marionetas.

Plazas que ceden como compuertas
al oleaje de la música.

Trenes que aúllan y nos reflejan
—como Platón—en cavernas

Rascacielos que nos raptan los ojos
hasta que nos pierden de vista.

Autopistas en que la muerte
arranca todos los días.

Mujeres que pasan y siembran

They inaugurate them with a party.
And they inhabit them, making love
for a while, and then,
little by little, war.

Until one day,
they're on their own,
they pack up and leave,
leaving the places alone
like a vacant stage
for those who no doubt will come
perhaps to stage
the same comedy.

*   *   *   *

CITY AT FIRST SIGHT

Two rivers like two arms
that embrace and enclose it.

Bridges that hang
and shine like bracelets.

Streets that rise and fall
just like the tide.

Neighborhoods that rise every morning
to the Pentecost of languages.

Parks where light and breeze
play like marionettes.

Plazas that, like floodgates, oblige
the waves of music.

Trains that howl and reflect us
—like Plato—in caverns

Skyscrapers that steal our eyes
till they lose sight of us.

Highways where death
starts its engine every day.

Women who pass and plant

la revelación y el enigma

frente al deseo que desfallece pero
cambia de objeto y se reanima.

Y la ciudad que fluye esculpida
estatua del movimiento.

*   *   *   *

NOCTURNO DE LOS PORTEROS

Atentos a nuestro paso,
nos abren la puerta,
nos rozan los hombros
con voz que desanclan
para hundirla de nuevo
en un largo silencio.

Y estoicamente nostálgicos
permanecen en su sitio,
plantados en la ardiente
paciencia de su oficio,
mirando a la calle,
silbando a ratos
—las manos en los bolsillos—
una canción que drene
la marea ascendente del hastío.

Y tenaces como Atlas
en su vigilia sostienen
el sueño de los niños,
el rito de los amantes,
el insomnio de los ancianos,
que yacen en cada edificio,
en cada cuarto de la ciudad
que fluye como un navío
partiendo las aguas de la noche
hacia las costas del alba
que ellos, delante, avizoran
con los párpados salobres
y la mirada alucinada
de los mascarones.

El paraguas de Manhattan

****

the revelation and the enigma

facing a desire that weakens but
changes focus and revives.

And the city that flows; a carved
statue of movement.

*   *   *   *

NOCTURNE OF THE DOORMEN

Alert to our passing,
they open the door,
they brush our shoulders
with a voice they weigh anchor
only to plunge it again
into a long silence.

And stoically nostalgic
they remain in their place,
planted in the ardent
patience of their task,
staring at the street,
whistling at times
—hands in pockets—
a song that might drain
the rising tide of boredom.

And tenacious as Atlas
on their watch they bear
the sleep of children,
the ritual of lovers,
the insomnia of the elderly
who lie in every building,
in every room of the city
that flows like a ship
parting the waters of the night
toward the coasts of dawn
that they, out ahead, are on alert for
with briny eyelids
and the hallucinated gaze
of hideous masks.

El paraguas de Manhattan

****

VITRAL DEL SUR

La ventana mira hacia el sur,
a una noche de invierno.

El viento corre sin parar
—sin pasar—
en las calaminas del techo.

Se adivinan afuera
las agujas del frío,
las alcachofas encapuchadas
por la nevada en el huerto.

En torno al brasero,
voces familiares
caen en arabescos,
crepitan en las brasas.

Un niño desde su cama
contempla cómo las sombras
en la pared de su cuarto
se achican y se agigantan.

Lentamente el sueño
le desancha la mirada
y lo transporta días,
noches, años abajo,
hasta otro cuarto donde
a la luz de una lámpara
un hombre encorvado
revive estas imágenes

y abrazo al precario
neumático de las palabras
se desvive hasta el alba
por evitar su naufragio.

*   *   *   *

VITRAL DEL PASADO

Nunca se quedó atrás nuestro pasado:
tenaz, centra intervalos de aparente olvido,
nos fue siguiendo los pasos, furtivo
como un ladrón detrás de los árboles.

THE SOUTH STAINED-GLASS WINDOW

The window faces south,
toward a wintry night.

The wind runs endlessly
—without passing—
through the roof's galvanized sheets.

Outside, one imagines
the needles of cold,
the artichokes hooded
by the snow in the garden.

Around the hearth,
familiar voices
fall in arabesques,
crackle in the hot coals.

From his bed, a little boy
contemplates how shadows
on the wall of his room
become smaller and then enormous.

Slowly sleep
narrows his gaze
and transports him days,
nights, years downstairs,
to another room where
under the light of a lamp
a hunched-over man
revives these images

and I embrace the precarious
inflated tire of words;
until dawn, it's anxious
to avoid its own shipwreck .

*   *   *   *

STAINED-GLASS WINDOW OF THE PAST

Our past never remained behind:
tenacious, it centers intervals of seeming oblivion,
it went on following our steps, furtive
like a thief behind the trees.

Pasajero invisible en los viajes,
se embarcó con nosotros
en los trenes y aviones
que por deseo o fuga abordamos

En los cuartos de los hoteles,
tras el azogue de los espejos
registró celestinamente
los cuerpos prohibidos que amamos.

A menudo, es cierto, perdió el sentido
(no las huellas) de nuestro tránsito,
 pero siguió, indigente, recolectando
fragmentos de cuanto vivimos.
Sólo bastó que llovieran los años
y nos volviéramos lentos
para sentirlo sobre la espalda, con su talego
de calamidades y milagros.

*   *   *   *

VITRAL ACÚSTICO

Sólo son voces y entran por la ventana,
siempre de noche, una por una
ocupan el cuarto, lo inundan,
de llantos, risas, plegarias.

Yo me desvelo por dibujarles
un cuerpo, una cara.
Pero apenas esbozo una línea,
unánimemente se callan.

Vitrales de la memoria

****

Invisible passenger on trips,
with us it boarded trains and planes
that we boarded willingly or to escape

In hotel rooms
behind the quicksilver of mirrors
it registered, like a procuress,
the forbidden bodies that we loved.

Often, it's true, it lost the sense
(not the tracks) of our journeys,
but it continued, indigent, collecting
fragments of all we live through.
All it took was for the years to rain down
on us and for us to slow down
to feel it on our back, with its sack
of calamities and miracles.

*   *   *   *

ACOUSTIC STAINED-GLASS WINDOW

They're only voices and they enter the window,
always at night, one by one
they occupy the room, they inundate it
with cries, laughter, prayers.

I stay up drawing them
a body, a face.
But as soon as I sketch a line,
they unanimously shut up.

Vitrales de la memoria

****

4

Jaime Nisttahuz

POEMA PARA UN POEMA

Hablando de huérfanos
una mujer acaba de orinar en media calle
aunque usted no lo crea
su mirada nos despreciaba junto a las paredes
las puertas la misma calle.
Tal vez usted hubiera intentado reprocharla
(si olvidaba su cobardía).
Con tal motivo he roto varios poemas
y he bebido un trago largo.
Es difícil creer en nosotros mismos
es difícil creer que ocurra un poema semejante
a esa mujer a media tarde
loca
rebelde
dueña del mundo
desafiando a la música de moda
desafiando como una flor a las piedras
sus aguas apenas mojaban unos veinte centímetros
veinte centímetros
¡toda una melodía!

Palabras con agujeros

****

CARTA

No sé desde cuándo
          he querido
escribirte desde dónde
ya sin exageraciones
          ni fatuidades.

Qué trabajo tan molesto
resultaba a ratos tu ausencia.
Y ese gris torpe de la distancia
tratando de ocultarme los colores
en pleno día.

¿Te quieren como buscabas?

El salto de tu risa en cualquier esquina
me partía en dos al oírte nombrar
tu piel me quemaba en mi piel

POEM FOR A POEM

Speaking of orphans
a woman just urinated in the middle of the street
even though you might not believe it
her look scorned us along with the walls
the doors and even the street.
Perhaps you might have intended to reproach her
(had you forgotten your cowardice.)
For this reason I've torn up several poems
and I've had a long drink.
It's difficult to believe in ourselves
it's difficult to believe that such a poem might occur
to that woman in the middle of the afternoon
crazy
rebellious
proprietress of the world
opposing trendy music
opposing like a flower to rocks
her puddle barely wet twenty centimeters
twenty centimeters
that makes a melody!

Palabras con agujeros

****

LETTER

I don't know since when
            I've wanted
to write you from wherever
without exaggerations
            nor fatuous remarks.

What a bothersome task your
absence has become at times.
And that clumsy gray of distance
trying to hide colors from me
in broad daylight.

Do they love you the way you wanted?

The suddenness of your laughter on any corner
hearing your name just cut me in two
your flesh burned my flesh

como si presintiera dolidamente
algunas noches
        un vacío.
¿Te han colmado la ansiedad?

A partir de cero tuve que empezar
a olvidarte más a menudo
hasta donde puede el olvido
para que los árboles y las calles
vuelvan a sonreírme
a una rosa
sea otra vez rosa.

*   *   *   *

MARCHA

Vivan los hombres inconformes.
Mueran los viejos adulones.
Caguen los ricos ignorantes.
Viva el que hiere a la injusticia.

Ya muchas lluvias la sonrisa me han mojado
y quiero hacerme de coraje un grito al cielo.

Muera andrajoso el egoísta incurable.
El blasón verdadero es la conciencia.
Vivan los niños que aprendieron de las calles.
La verdad es la consigna.

Ya muchas lluvias la sonrisa me han mojado
y quiero hacerme de coraje un grito al cielo.

*   *   *   *

RETRATO

Merodea los cincuenta.

Licenciado en ciencias económicas.
Se ha iniciado discretamente
llevando contabilidades menores
para tiendas y cafetines.

Siempre la vida le ha parecido
una gradería que subir

as if I painfully foresaw
on some nights
                    a void.
Have they calmed your anxiety?

Starting from zero I had to begin
forgetting you more often
as far as forgetting is able
so that the trees and streets
smile again at me
and for a rose
to be, once again, a rose.

*   *   *   *

A MARCH

Long live the non-conformists.
Death to the old ass-kissers.
Shit on the ignorant rich guys.
Long live those who wound injustice.

Many bitter rains have dampened my smile
and I want to vent my rage shouting at heaven.

Let the incurable egotist die ragged.
The true badge is the conscience.
Long live the kids who became street wise.
Truth is the watchword.

Many bitter rains have dampened my smile
and I want to vent my rage shouting to heaven.

*   *   *   *

PORTRAIT

He's plundering fifty.

A degree in economics.
he began discreetly
handling minor accounts
for stores and cafés.

Life has always seemed to him
a staircase for moving up

sin cargos de conciencia.

Es en la actualidad
puntual insustituible del Estado
según él.

Muestra su casa con orgullo.

Su automóvil es parte de su corbata.
Piensa que las mujeres
le sonríen más allá de su traje.

Habla hasta por los codos
y promete por vivos y muertos.

Siempre cree saber más que el otro
y sonríe con los ojos.

En sus largos viajes ha observado
GRANDES COSAS

y como su alma no ha crecido
la ignora con astucia deslumbrante.
Paz—orden—trabajo es su divisa.
Acaba de pasar
saludando como un campeón.

                    Escrito en los muros

*   *   *   *

INTIMIDAD

Se me ocurrió hoy buscarte
como si no estuvieras en todas las esquinas
                    (de mis manos
con tus nombre más íntimos
y he querido contar a los árboles
                    a las piedras
                    a la lluvia
lo que dices cuando partimos
sobre el color de nuestra piel
envolviéndonos como olas
aturdiendo al mundo en una ebriedad de luz
deslumbrado lo que nos mira
cuando hasta el aire parece crujir

with no pangs of conscience.

At present, he is
an indispensable stanchion of the State
according to him.

He shows off his house with pride.

His car is part of his necktie.
He thinks that women
smile at him beyond his suit.

He chatters incessantly, making
promises for the living and the dead.

He always believes he knows more than
the next guy and he smiles with his eyes.

On his long trips, he's observed
GREAT THINGS

and since his soul hasn't grown
he ignores it with blinding astuteness.
Peace—order—work is his motto.
He just passed by
waving like a champion.

Escrito en los muros

*   *   *   *

INTIMACY

It occurred to me to look for you today
as if you weren't in every corner
                    (of my hands
with your most intimate names
and I've wanted to tell the trees
                    the rocks
                    the rain
what you say when we part
about the color of our skin
wrapping around us like waves
bewildering the world in a drunken light
dazzled, all who see us
when even the air seems to crackle

al calor de nuestras palabras
y es como si estuviéramos en un bosque
de tus ojos
y mis ojos
donde las paredes
se pierden
donde rugen y cantan
fieras y dioses antiguos
en nuestra sed.

El murmullo de las ropas

*   *   *   *

AFÁN

Soy como un viejo obstinado
discutiendo con perros en la calle
en este afán
a media tarde
cuando el cielo
                    y las nubes
                    con su esplendor
                                    logran perfilar
              a brochazos
este mundo
a media sonrisa
en el dibujo
que no hice todavía
como si un niño
a media tos
golpeara el hierro
de tantas dudas
golpeándome
dentro
los sentimientos
los pensamientos
disintiendo
como perros en la calle.

La humedad es una sombra...

*   *   *   *

to the warmth of our words
as if we were in a forest
of your eyes
and my eyes
where walls
disappear
where ancient beasts and gods
roar and sing
in our thirst.

El murmullo de las ropas

*   *   *   *

ANXIETY

I'm like an obstinate old man
arguing with dogs in the street
in this anxiety
in mid afternoon
when the sky
          and the clouds
          with their splendor
              are able to polish
      with brushstrokes
this world
half smiling
in the drawing
that I haven't done yet
as if a child
half coughing
were to strike the iron
of so many doubts
striking me
within
my feelings
my thoughts
dissenting
like dogs in the street.

La humedad es una sombra...

*   *   *   *

TRANSFORMACIÓN

si un poema
para florecer o volar
tiene que partir de golpearme contra la pared
de embrutecerme bebiendo
o de acunarlo
como a un niño
no es un poema
son palabras recordando el dibujo
de un caballo que salta
dentro
de mí
      y sale de vez en cuando
como un mendigo.

*   *   *   *

REITERANDO LAS CALLES DE NUESTRA PIEL

Malbaratamos nuestra vida
otros la regatean.
          Como un fantasma
la mujer
que dejamos
provoca nuestras dudas.
La que nos deja
es una bestia
que prosigue
devorando
nuestra
ropa
interior.

La mujer
que nos pierde
tiene otro hueso.
Aquella
que perdimos
es un sendero que no terminamos de caminar.

*   *   *   *

TRANSFORMATION

if a poem
in order to flower or to fly has to depart
from slamming me against the wall
from brutalizing me by drinking
or from cradling it
like a child
it's not a poem
they are words recalling the drawing
of a horse that leaps
inside
of me
     and comes out from time to time
like a beggar.

*   *   *   *

REITERATING THE STREETS OF OUR SKIN

We squander our lives
others bargain for it.
                Like a ghost
the woman
that we leave
provokes our doubts.
The one who leaves us
is a beast
that proceeds
to devour
our
under
wear.

The woman
who causes our ruin
has another story.
That one,
the one we lost
is a path that we will never finish walking.

*   *   *   *

COMO UN PUNTO

En busca de ese poema
que comienza y termina en sí mismo
voy extraviándome entre estas piedras.
Y ese poema (estoy seguro) es tan corto
que se parece al último aliento
o al primer grito.
Tan exacto
como una puñalada sin remedio
tan posible
como caminar sobre agua.

*   *   *   *

ATRAPADOS

ciegos a un cielo
                          pulido por el viento
hostigados por el mañana
agobiados por el ayer
aguardamos un
                          eco
sin poder salir
de nuestra sombra

Recodo en el aire

****

LIKE A DOT

In search of that poem
that begins and ends in itself,
I'm going astray among these rocks.
And that poem (I am sure) is so short
that it seems like the last breath
or the first cry.
So exact
like a knife stab without hope
so possible
like walking on water.

*   *   *   *

TRAPPED

blind to a sky
        polished by the wind
whipped by the future
overwhelmed by the past
we retain an
        echo
without being able to leave
our own shadow.

Recodo en el aire

****

5

Eduardo Nogales

BAR AVERNO

Duerme un demonio en la espuma y el tejado
Y lo que fue barro se hace un barco destrozado en la mesa
En el que viajamos hacia el centro de aquella llovizna
Detenida por un perro bizco

Los callejones nos persiguen
La palabra nos maldice
La única luz es una puerta donde nos espera
Una mujer loca

Encapuchados con la ciudad oscura recolectamos arañas
Para que nos abriguen
La ciudad está al borde de la niebla
Y parece que ha estallado una guerra en nuestra ausencia
Ah
            Desventurados danzantes
Alguien dejó un hedor distinto al gusano
Alguien se llevó el negro musgo de las casas
Alguien dejó otra vez el mundo apagado en este sitio.

La nave iluminada

****

El patio ha conseguido su inquietud
En las goteras
Como mi vida.

*   *   *   *

Dije al conocerte
Lo que habita en el silencio es perpetuo

Y no hay quien diga
Sigue allí lo que llueve

No intentes un recuerdo
Mira esta vida
No dejes pasar lo que se alcanza tarde.

Los deseantes del arca

****

THE AVERNO BAR

A demon sleeps upon foam and the roof
What was once clay becomes a wrecked ship on the table
The ship we travel on toward the center of that drizzle
A drizzle detained by a cross-eyed dog

The alleys pursue us
The word curses us
The only light is a door where
A crazy woman awaits us

Heads hooded with a dark city, we collect spiders
So they can shelter us
The city is at the edge of the fog
And it seems a war has broken out in our absence
Ah
          Unfortunate dancers
Someone left a stench different from the worm's
Someone took away the black moss of the houses
Someone again left the world extinguished in this place.

La nave iluminada

****

The patio has fetched its restiveness
From drippings
Like my life.

*   *   *   *

Upon meeting you I said
That what resides in silence is perpetual

And no one will say
That whatever the rain brings will remain

Don't attempt a memory
Look at this life
Don't let what is belatedly achieved pass by.

Los deseantes del arca

****

64

El desierto es un sabio indiferente
Recluido en la alejada admiración de la vida
Y en el abandono de los veloces caminos

Aquí
Nada igual que la emoción de los últimos amores
Llenos de arena
Proscritos en la infancia
Para designar en la mirada
La consigna de la luna
Y la voluntad de las quimeras.

*   *   *   *

El imperio del mundo
Es insignificante en un desierto

Lo humano es incompetente
En reconocer las rutas verdaderas.

*   *   *   *

Junto al estupor del adivino
El sitio más bello del imposible aquí
Como si todo recién estuviera
En el pensamiento

En esta vasta situación
Es inútil mentir
Que un designio ha señalado del hombre
Este todo
Y de todo este Dios

Parece un mandamiento agradecer
La obra del silencio
Valdría poco la resignación

Aquí
Nada hay
Sólo piedra sobre piedra enraizada
En lo oscuro.
Quién sería esta vida?

El jardín de las lentitudes

****

The desert is an indifferent wise man
Reclusive in its distant admiration of life
And in the abandonment of high-speed roads

Here
Nothing can match the thrill of the last loves
Filled with sand
Banished in infancy
To assign in one's gaze
The watchword of the moon
and the will of the chimeras.

*   *   *   *

The empire of the world
Is insignificant in the desert

The human way is incompetent
In recognizing the true paths.

*   *   *   *

Next to the prophet's wonder
The most beautiful place of the impossible here
As if everything just came to mind

In this vast arrangement
It's useless to lie
That from man some design
has determined this all
And from this all, this God

It appears to be a commandment
To thank the work of silence
Resignation would be worth little

Here
There's nothing
Only stone upon rooted stone
In the dark.
Whose life would this be?

El jardín de las lentitudes

****

Humo de luna
Sobre la última noche de Borges*
Azar de la mancha de los tigres
No su corazón desprevenido por el que muy pocas mujeres
        llegaron
Exentas de amor
Cuyo aroma llevaría la sentencia del arrabal y el tango
Ese himno decadente de las estrellas
Que en los espejos del fango
No sería más que la memoria del alcohol y de las lunas
        que afamaron la vida

Desde entonces y para negar las ilusiones
A pesar de la cifra de los atardeceres y los libros
La tierra sería una taberna
Un arrabal
y una letra más entre las cosas y los símbolos.

*Jorge Luis Borges,célebre poeta,cuentista y
    ensayista argentino (1899-1986).

*   *   *   *

Y perseguiré esa nube
Y cada atardecer será una ofrenda a la eternidad de los
        dinosaurios
A la fábula de los amores arruinados
A las cartas escritas a medianoche y que los fantasmas
        ávidos esperan
En las extrañas rutas
Hasta devorar la deliciosa certidumbre de los amantes
y dejar que el aroma de los besos insatisfechos
Vuelvan a las alcobas donde desovaron los incautos
        Su esperanza
Junto al tenue brillo del cielo que nunca alcanzaron.

*   *   *   *

Volver es aniquilar el animal del recuerdo

En el regreso
Una infancia de pronto acude a la posesión de lo que no
        se ha ido

Tal vez el corazón es el instante y el instrumento
Que reserva el ángel

Lunar smoke
Above the last night of Borges*
The misfortune of the tigers' blemish
Not his unprepared heart, for which very few
        women came forth, exempt from love,
Whose aroma would carry along the essence of
slums and tangos
The decadent hymn of the stars
That in the mirrors of the mire
Wouldn't be more than the memory of alcohol and
        the moons that celebrated life

Since then and to deny any illusions
In spite of the number of sunsets and books
Life would be a tavern
A slum
and one more letter among things and symbols.

*Jorge Luis Borges, World-famous Argentine poet, narrative
    writer and essayist (1899-1986).

*   *   *   *

And I will pursue that cloud
And every sunset will be an offering to the
        eternity of the dinosaurs
To the fable of ruined loves
To the letters written at midnight; those that
        ghosts avidly await
On their strange routes
Until devouring the delicious certainty of lovers
and permitting the aroma of unsatisfied kisses
To return to bedrooms where the unwary spawned
        their hope
Next to the thin brilliance of the sky they never reached.

*   *   *   *

To return is to annihilate the animal of memory

In the return
An infancy soon presents itself to the
        possession of what has not departed

Perhaps the heart is the instant and the instrument
That the angel reserves

A los castigados de la noche

Volver es un niño que nos alcanza en todo el cuerpo
Hasta encontrar el río de la lengua
Donde la inocencia arrojará la luna entera y masacrada
A los reflejos cambiantes de la vida alegre

Pero la infancia es el dominio que fecunda el castigo
Y el castigo a la vez es la perpetuidad de la inocencia

Todo ángel nos revela esa condición del asombro.

El último cabaret

****

En la noche de la selva
Junto al mojado templo de los ojos solos
Pasa una golondrina
Infantil navío que no tiene prisa
Ni la bruma ajada
Ni el camino a cuestas
Ni el oráculo que las antiguas razas
Inútilmente levantaron.

*   *   *   *

En este bello día de la vida
El rumor de las hojas
Evocan mi pertenencia

Pero nada se acostumbra en mí
Entonces ando por las orillas
Tras las goteras del envejecido patio
Atento a la golondrina
Ella que vuelve con su corazón de musgo
Que no espera nada más que jugar
En el barco luminoso de su regreso.

*   *   *   *

Cuando miro mi aldea
Quiero irme por otras calles menos ciertas de este
mundo
Y trazo el color de mi barco
Arreglo mis cosa

For those punished at night

To return is a child that takes hold of our entire bodies
Until finding the river of the tongue
Where innocence will hurl the full, bloodied moon
At the mutating reflections of the merry life

But infancy is the domain that inseminates punishment
And punishment in turn is the perpetuity of innocence

Every angel reveals to us that nature of amazement.

El ultimo cabaret

****

In the night of the jungle
Next to the damp temple of the lonely eyes
A dove passes
A childlike ship that is in no hurry
Nor the tarnished fog
Nor the up-and-down road
Nor the oracle that ancient races
Uselessly erected.

*   *   *   *

On this beautiful day of life
The rustle of the leaves
Evokes my belonging here

But nothing in me gets accustomed to it
So I chase after drippings
On the edges of the aged patio
Watchful of the dove
The one who returns with her heart of moss
That expects nothing more than to play
On the luminous ship of its return

*   *   *   *

When I look at my village
I want to leave for other, less certain streets of
this world
And I plan the color of my ship
I arrange my things

Beso el lugar donde fui feliz
Y saldo mi penumbra.

*   *   *   *

Tendría fin la poesía
Si el silencio acabaría
La bulla evita la inteligencia y la interpretación

Poesía es traducir de los dioses
Lo que callan

Sólo la palabra que interpreta y traduce el silencio
A la vez preserva a los dioses

Tal la terrible hermosura
Y la custodia final
De toda poesía.

El humo del paraíso

****

I kiss the place where I was happy
And I sell off my penumbra.

*   *   *   *

Poetry will see its ending
If silence were to end
Noise avoids intelligence and interpretation

Poetry is translating from the gods
All that they keep silent

Only the word interprets and translates silence
At the same time preserving the gods

Such the terrible beauty
And the final custody
Of all poetry.

El humo del paraíso

****

6

Juan Carlos Orihuela

PRÓLOGO

Fermento de la memoria tendida
arena dispersa que profana su reverso.
Entras dejando abierta la puerta
mostrándome la extensión descuartizada del tiempo
que intenta
—como el agua—
resolver su cuerpo
en la dificultad.

Tocándote
recorreré los nudos formados
para que la materia fugaz del sueño se revele
en palabras y sonidos
que tal vez ni quieran adivinar la procedencia
de tu piel lastimada.

Entenderé que no llegas con la mirada puesta
en la línea efímera del transcurso
y que la más oculta de tus palabras viene a recuperar
sin insistencia
el lugar en que se clausura la historia
antes de volver a repetirse.

Sólo entonces pedirás rescatar los secretos de los cuervos
mudándose en otoño
mientras inscribas tu teología en la noche
de sus cuerpos colgados.

Yo me olvidaré en la percepción de tus miradas
cada vez que desde los dientes de la ciudad
solicites no ser descubierta
ni por sus corrientes subterráneas
ni por sus orificios de entrada.

Quizás luego alguien se conozca en el humo de tus ojos
y pueda orar por última vez
frente a la orilla elegida por los ríos
para morir pronto.

Desde el lugar señalado
donde acaece la luz de la tarde
recordarás tu nombre enredado entre los nombres
para dejar que los muertos entierren a sus muertos
y se te haga menos penoso lo aprendido a la sombra

PROLOGUE

A ferment of memory stretched out
scattered sand that profanes its reverse.
You enter leaving the door open
showing me the quartered extension of time
that attempts
—like water—
to resolve its body
in difficulty.

Touching you
I'll go over the formed knots
to reveal the dream's fleeting material
in words and sounds
that perhaps refuse to guess the origin
of your injured flesh.

I'll understand that you don't come with a gaze fixed
on the ephemeral line of the passage of time
and the most hidden of your words comes to recoup
without insistence
the place in which history closes
before repeating itself.

Only then will you ask to rescue the crows' secrets
moving in the autumn
while you inscribe your theology in the night
of their hanging bodies.

I'll forget as I perceive your glances
every time that, from the teeth of the city,
you request not to be discovered
not by its subterranean currents
nor by its orifices of entry.

Perhaps later someone can know himself in the haze
of your eyes and can pray for the last time
facing the shore chosen by the rivers
to die quickly.

From the chosen place
where the afternoon light happens
you'll remember your name tangled among names
to leave the dead bury the dead and
everything learned might distress you less in the shadow

de sus grietas.

Menos mal que vienes a decirme desde la región remota
donde habitas entre cartas de conjuro
y animales de todas las edades.
Menos mal que llegas a alertarme con tu cuerpo renacido
pasando de un canto al otro
entre danzas de fuego y de caballo
para que yo no sienta más el temor del que llega al mundo
con el culo al aire.

*   *   *   *

Los cuerpos se reconocen en los cuerpos
   no son pasajeros

Están ahí diciendo y contando
   son siempre una pasión cíclica que funda
la única comunidad posible después de la unidad.

Los cuerpos se transmiten
   se consiguen alrededor de cosas sueltas
que se impiden el paso olvidándose de sí.

Todo en ellos semeja gotas en descaro por donde
descienden las sombras de otros cuerpos
intentando justificar sus alianzas
en el fastidio
   como si el roce o el tacto no fueran suficientes.

En los cuerpos perviven las constelaciones
   los rencores
el desdén
   la fe
la poca monta   la corona
   las palabras no deseadas.

En los cuerpos se predice el olvido
y el tiempo de la holganza suele ser el anticipo
de una historia contada en la insubordinación
de una mirada que se reconoce en las aguas
con cautela.

Provistos de un pudor cercano al odio
los cuerpos son siempre el exceso
   lo no hecho

of its cracks.

It's better that you come from a remote region to tell me
where you dwell among conspiratorial letters
and animals of all ages.
It's better that you come to alert me with your reborn body
passing from one song to the other
between dances of fire and of horses
so I no longer feel the fear of those who come into the world
butt first.

    *   *   *   *

Bodies recognize each other in bodies
        they are not transient

They are over there saying and telling
        they are always a cyclical passion founding
the only community possible after unity.

Bodies are transmitted
        they are obtained around scattered things
that are prevented from entry, being left behind.

Everything in them seems like impudent drops
through which the shadows of other bodies descend
attempting to justify their alliances
in weariness
        as if rubbing or touching weren't sufficient.

In bodies, things survive: constellations
        grudges
disdain
        faith
insignificance   the crown
        unwanted words.

Forgetfulness is predicted in bodies
and the time of idleness tends to be the anticipation
of a story told in the insubordination
of a look that is recognized with astuteness
in the seas.

Armed with a modesty neighboring on hatred
bodies are always the excess
        what was not done

78

o lo hecho hasta decir basta.

Los cuerpos son las lágrimas soberbias
de las maldiciones y de las reverencias
        que se desbordan en los filos
hasta que un brazo los recoge y alimenta
y entonces
        parias
los cuerpos se encogen y se dejan llevar
        mansos
hasta sus impredecibles refugios.

Los cuerpos pasan por el mundo
intercambiando obsequios
        inscribiéndose a sí mismos como un tatuaje mutuo
que los hace mirarse en los espejos y conocerse en
las miradas de las fieras y las aves.

Son la innecesaria reverencia del gesto oblicuo
        un corte de sesgo en el recuerdo de otros cuerpos
que les salieron al paso para narrarles las cenizas
de otros cuerpos que optaron por una caída abierta
y ya no volvieron.

Los cuerpos son el centro del remordimiento.

Cuerpos del cuerpo

****

TRANSCURSOS   I

Se dice que los ríos fundaron el tiempo.
Los subterráneos
                los claros
los no encontrados
                los desconocidos
los fétidos
        anunciaron el tiempo
—dice.

Alguna edad también los recuerda apoyados
en los árboles
        hablando con las laderas o el fuego
vaciando sus lágrimas en las orillas
antes de continuar agitándose por las corrientes

or what was done until we say enough.

Bodies are the haughty tears
of the curses and reverences
        that overflow edges
until an arm collects and feeds them
and then
        pariahs
bodies shrink and are led off
            meekly
to their unpredictable retreats.

Bodies pass through the world
exchanging gifts
        inscribing one another like a mutual tattoo
forcing them to see each other in mirrors and
be known in the sights of beasts and birds.

They are the unnecessary reverence of an oblique gesture
            a slanted cut in the memory of other bodies
who intercepted them to narrate the ashes
of other bodies that opted for an open fall
and no longer returned.

Bodies are the center of remorse.

Cuerpos del cuerpo

****

PASSAGES OF TIME, I

It is said that rivers founded time.
The subterranean ones
                the clear ones
the ones not found
                the unknown ones
the fetid ones
        they all announced time
—so they say.

Another age also remembers them leaning
against trees
        conversing with the hillsides or the fire
emptying their tears on the shores
before moving on and getting rough in the currents

y los cauces
      y las cavernas.

Ya tierra amarga
      ya ciénaga
a los ríos les fue encomendada
la configuración de las texturas
del mundo.
Sus hilos horadaron pacientemente
la piel ambigua del planeta
y se dispersaron como finas cicatrices
por su esqueleto imaginado
      —estrías aprendiendo
el lugar de las nuevas especies
      rumores hondos
          remotos
cavando por debajo.

En el oficio de los ríos procrearon
las lagunas y los estanques
reposando sus algas y sus bejucos
en el inicio de los abrevaderos
      anunciando su muerte en el
          devenir ciego
revolcándose frente a los remolinos
en demanda de piel mutua
cuando es noche y pasan los camalotes
y bogan incansables raíces
      sedimentos.

*   *   *   *

LÍTICA

Así como tu vida
      piedra
como la mía que atraviesa
      lunar
          la tuya.

Morando como tú
      clandestina
hierba de los instintos
      peregrina que se detuvo
como nosotros
entre piedras que estuvieron

and in the riverbeds
   and in the caverns.

Now yellow soil
   now swamps
rivers were entrusted with
the configuration of the textures
of the world.
Their thin streams patiently hollowed out
the ambiguous skin of the planet
and dispersed like fine scars
along its imagined skeleton
   —grooves learning
the place of new species
   deep murmurs
     remote
digging through underneath.

In the occupation of the rivers they procreated
lagoons and pools
placing their algae and their reeds
at the source of the watering places
   announcing their death in the
      blind flux
rolling about before the whirlpools
in demand of a mutual skin
when it's night and the water hyacinths pass through
and skim untiring roots
    sediments.

 *   *   *   *

LITHIC

Just as with your life
   a stone
like mine that crosses
   moonlike
     yours.

Dwelling like you do
   clandestinely
an herb of the instincts
   a pilgrim that stopped
like we did
among stones that were

82

en lo remoto de la hoguera.

Lápida de los corales
    de los carbones
        de espejo a espejo
de tiempo a tiempo
    en la lenta y hermosa
        rutina de los días.

*   *   *   *

RETORNOS

Para amarte había preparado un lienzo
        y una cerbatana.
Había también mirado el sesgo de tu falda
   —penúltimo corcel de mi estampida—
para que tus ojos inicien sus murmullos
y desciendan serenando las horas nuevas.

Algo así como un astro se apoyaba
en mis costados
    algo así como una garúa
descendiendo por las oquedades
        de mi infancia.

Oficio de tiempo

****

in the remoteness of the bonfire.

Gravestone of corals
     of coals
         from mirror to mirror
from time to time
     in the slow and beautiful
         routine of the days.

*   *   *   *

RETURNINGS

To love you, I had prepared a canvas
     and a pea shooter.
I had also peered at the slant of your skirt
   —the penultimate steed of my stampede—
for your eyes to initiate their sighing
and to descend serenading the new hours.

Something like a star was reclining
on my sides
     something like a fine drizzle
descending through the hollowness
         of my infancy.

Oficio de tiempo

****

7

Humberto Quino

PINTA LO QUE LE SUCEDE A UN POETA
SIN HALO / CON QUERIDA Y SIN MELENA

Es demasiado para cualquiera
Sostener la lira / L bacinilla
Comer higos secos en verano
Verduras
O
Dejarse crecer la barba
                    Las uñas
                    Los cabellos
O
Pesar el tintineo de sus huesos
En cuclillas
De pie
O
Echado sobre un colchón de paja.

Balada para mi coronel. . .

****

A PROPÓSITO DE NUESTRO
MAL / NATURAL REPOLLO

Para que el pan
Sea un bocado común
Para que la blasfemia
Vaya en carroza
En fin
Para suprimir los golpes de estado
Hay que suprimir el estado.

El diablo predicador

****

HIMNO GUERRERO O LAS SEÑAS
DE UNA RAZÓN INÚTIL

Sólo poseo la pesadilla
Su alquimia / Su carbón
Arcana belleza / Escalera oscura
De la muerte mudo espejo.

yo soy Humberto Quino

DESCRIBING WHAT HAPPENS TO A POET
WITHOUT A HALO / WITH A SWEETHEART
AND WITHOUT A PONY TAIL

It's too much for anyone
Holding up the lyre / D chamber pot
Eating dry figs in the summer
Greens
Or
Let your beard grow
       Finger nails
       Hair
Or
Weigh the clinking of your bones
Squatting
On foot
Or
Lying on a straw mattress.

Balada para mi coronel

****

CONCERNING OUR ILLNESS/NATURAL CABBAGE

In order for bread
To be a common mouthful
In order for blasphemy
To go in a hearse
In short
In order to suppress coups d'état
You have to suppress the state.

El Diablo predicador

****

WARRIOR HYMN OR THE SIGNS
OF A USELESS REASON

I only possess the nightmare
It's alchemy / It's coal
An arcane beauty / A dark staircase
Of death, a mute mirror.

I am Humberto Quino

Mensajero del mal
Sin espuelas / Sin anteojos
La cordura me aprieta.

Yo soy vuestro funámbulo
Hondo eclipse / Caído sin duelo
Yo te oigo / Tiempo vacío / Ídolo sombrío
Respirar en la altiplanicie / Condenado al delirio.

En mitad de la noche
Una ciudad de piedras me habita
La tuberculosis / Perros muertos
y es / Como mirar degollados
Braseros aniquilados / Esqueletos.

Y aún creo en la historia
Vieja leprosa
Alumbraré tu memoria / Sierva arrugada
Con clavos y flores.

Ésta es / Será mi hazaña.

Manual de esclavos

****

PATRIA DE POETA CAUTIVO

I
Brilla la soberbia
Y luego se apaga
En un lamento de sirena.

II
Y así aparece esta ciudad adorada por el vicio
Por las garrapatas y los funcionarios
En tanto / tu osario
En esa alta ladera de arena
palabras y piedra
Sapiencia y seda
Mas / polvo sobre polvo.

III
Tus musas secaron sus ubres
El poeta se peinó con pensamientos
Así es la ira que desaira.

Messenger of bad news
Without spurs / Without eyeglasses
Prudence cramps my style.

I am your tight-rope walker
Full eclipse / Fallen without mourners
I hear you / Empty time / Dark idol
Breathing in the high plateau / Condemned to delirium.

In the middle of the night
A stone city dwells within me
Tuberculosis / Dead dogs
and it is / like seeing decapitated people
Annihilated braziers / Skeletons.

And I still believe in history
Old leper
I will illuminate your memory / withered slave
with nails and flowers.

This is / will be my feat.

Manual de esclavos

****

COUNTRY OF A CAPTIVE POET

I
Pride shines
And later it dies out
in a siren's lament.

II
And so this city appears adored by vice
By ticks and by functionaries
Meanwhile / your ossuary
On that tall, sandy hillside
words and stone
Wisdom and silk
But / dust upon dust.

III
Your muses dried their udders
The poet combed himself with thoughts
Such is ire that rebuffs.

IV
Y llamar al poeta pan
Al pan poeta
para que las palabras vivan y sueñen
Para que las palabras no muerdan / No acaricien.

V
Yo también cuento fábulas.

Tratado sobre la superstición. . .

****

UN SANTO DE TU DEVOCIÓN

a Claudia

Aun espero la noche
Con una marca de sangre en la frente
y cuando la hora más ardiente llegue hasta mi nuca
y aún cuando yo muerto entre las ratas
Alabo tu hermosura
Para que me ilumine tu belleza
En este juego de amar y morir
En la nada.

*   *   *   *

CELEBRACIÓN DE UN INFANTE

Mi infancia era un humo azul
Un punto ciego en el cuarto escarlata
El mago Tou Fou acariciaba mis cabellos
Mi padre cabalgaba sobre mi vieja cuna
Como si estuviera fuera el mundo y su pesadumbre
Mi madre medusa comía una naranja
Su pálida tristeza me hundía en la gracia
En esa espuma desconocida y áspera que sería mi destino.

Mi infancia era una selva de sombreros y falacias
Querubín luciferino / Mi gloria era el infierno
El esqueleto de un caballo
Y ese hueco en la niebla donde una maldición tejía
Ya el telón había caído sobre mi razón
y sólo tenía la certeza
De haber sido echado del paraíso

IV
And calling the poet a spade
And the spade a poet
so that words can live and dream
So that words don't bite/ Don't caress.

V
I, too, tell fables.

Tratado sobre la superstición...

****

A SAINT OF YOUR DEVOTION

for Claudia

I'm still waiting for the night
With a spot of blood on my forehead
and when the most passionate hour comes to my nape
and even when I'm dead among the rats
I'll praise your fairness
So that your beauty will illuminate me
In this game of loving and dying
In nothingness.

*   *   *   *

CELEBRATION OF AN INFANT

My infancy was a blue haze
A blind dot in the scarlet room
The magician Tou Fou caressing my hair
My father riding horseback on my old cradle
As if he were outside the world and its sorrows.
My medusa mother eating an orange
Her pale sadness destroyed me in grace
In that unknown, gruff foam that would be my destiny.

My infancy was a jungle of hats and fallacies
A Luciferian cherub / My glory was hell
The horse's skeleton
And that hole in the fog where a curse was weaving
Already, the curtain had fallen on my reason
and I was only sure
Of having been thrown from paradise

Entonces / Me desaté la lengua
Me rompí un brazo
Y me masturbé como un simio.

Crítica de la pasión pura

****

A LA ALTURA DE TUS LABIOS

Mi mujer cava una fosa
Y tiene la forma de una boca roja
Mi mujer cava una fosa
Muda y flaca y oscura.
Bebemos la leche de la noche
Es la sed del ahorcado
Su reloj de tristeza
Su vaso de vino con migaja
Su incinerado amor
Por eso escribo / Amada serpiente.

Summa poética

****

HÓRRIDO CLAUSTRO ES MI ASADURA

Amo a esas mujeres que la noche fecunda
Que la oscuridad devora
y el alcohol sus vientres mordisquea.

Amo esa madrugada
En que la ronca queja
Creció entre mi pelo blanco
Por la muerta y su miseria de baraja.

Amo ese cuerpo de sol naciente
Su laica desnudez como una espina
Su balar de bestia enfurecida
Saber que ella será cuando yo ya no sea más.

Amo esa arteria de la desdicha
Sentada en mi mirada con su tajeada belleza
Caracol y hollín del desencanto
Guijarro que acribilla la ceremonia de la vida.

Then I loosened my tongue
I broke my arm
And I masturbated like an ape.

Crítica de la passion pura

****

LEVEL WITH YOUR LIPS

My wife digs a grave
And it's shaped like a red mouth
My wife digs a grave
Mute and skinny and dark.
We drink in the evening's milk
It's the thirst of a hanged man
His clock of sadness
His glass of wine with crumbs
His incinerated love
That's why I write / Beloved serpent.

Summa poética

****

A HORRID CLOISTER ARE MY INNARDS

I love those women spawned by the night
Whom darkness devours
and alcohol nibbles at their bellies.

I love that daybreak
When a hoarse cry
Grew within my white hair
For the dead woman and the misery dealt to her.

I love that body of the rising sun
Her secular nudity like a thorn
Her braying like a furious beast
Knowing she will be when I no longer am.

I love that artery of misfortune
Seated within my gaze with her chiseled beauty
A snail and soot of disenchantment
A pebble that riddles the ceremony of life.

Amo la poesía herida de muerte
Su desquiciado rostro que aniquila el desamparo
Su maligno tacto de animal en celo
Su incandescencia que me devuelve a la vida.

Pero amar es caer bajo su designio
Que engendra / Hiere y mata.

*   *   *   *

CARPE DIEM

En la mesa de la vida
Somos arrojados por un dios-hembra.
Inflamados por la muerte
Que por dentro anda
Esperando el último repique
El vómito que nos devuelva a la nada.

*   *   *   *

YACE AQUÍ LA DESNUDA QUE AMOR FUE

Ahora que la ciudad arde
De las cenizas nazco
Para contemplar esa herida que amor fue.
Para contemplar esa hierba que amor fue.

Y devora insectos y mujeres
En esta choza de gusanos.

*   *   *   *

CUANDO PERDI MI CHAQUETA EN UNA CUEVA
DONDE EL MACHO CABRIO ERA DIOS

Estaba ebrio en una ciudad extraña
con mis resquebrajadas alas
Como un espectro predicando el evangelio
Era un manso animal de húmeda cabeza
magro en la gris calle
Héroe de perdida patria.

Crítica de la pasión pura

****

I love poetry wounded by death
Its disturbing face annihilates helplessness
Its malignant touch of an animal in heat
Its incandescence that brings me back to life.

But to love is to fall under its design
That engenders / hurts, and kills.

*   *   *   *

CARPE DIEM

Onto the table of life
We are thrown by a she-god.
Inflamed by death
That walks inside of us
Waiting for the last tolling of the bell
The vomit that returns us to nothingness.

*   *   *   *

HERE LIES THE NUDE THAT LOVE WAS

Now that the city burns
From ashes I am born
To contemplate that wound that love was.
To contemplate that grass that love was.

And it devours insects and women
In this hut of worms.

*   *   *   *

WHEN I LOST MY JACKET IN A CAVE WHERE THE MALE GOAT WAS GOD

I was drunk in a strange city
With my cracked wings
Like a specter preaching the gospel
It was a tame animal with a wet head
Gaunt in the gray street
A hero of a lost country.

Crítica de la pasión pura

****

OYE LADRAR A LOS POETAS DE PRESA

Su gloria es esta ratonera alborotada
Estas grises historias inscritas en el olvido
Estas almas que su cruz clavaron en una carcajada.

Sembraron el olor de la bestia debajo su piel
Se astillaron los huesos
Sorbieron venenos y pócimas.

Sobre ellos un cuervo llora
Su irrisoria vida
Su verso de seda.

¿Dónde ocultar mi rostro
Si ya está pintado mi epitafio?

Coitus ergo sum

****

LISTEN TO THE BARKING OF
THE POETS OF PREY

Their glory is this excited mousetrap
These gray stories inscribed in oblivion
These souls that nailed their cross to a guffaw.

The smell of a beast was planted under their skin
Their bones were splintered
They sipped on poisons and potions.

Above them cries a crow
Its laughable life
Its silky verses.

Where can I hide my face
If my epitaph is already painted?

Coitus ergo sum

****

8

María Soledad Quiroga

INTEMPERIE

Un árbol en medio de la calle
entre los automóviles lúcidos
y los oscuros transeúntes
de riguroso perfil
lanza discursos floridos
al humo que los devora.

*   *   *   *

DESFILADERO

Sobre
el puro abismo
cortado desde el cielo
la pendiente limpia
sin piedras ni estorbos vegetales
sólo viento atravesado
en la garganta
sólo oscuridad incubada
largamente.
En la cima
trepando sobre sí
aire esforzado sobre aire
y espuma de acero
se eleva frágil y osada
la estructura del vacío.

*   *   *   *

CIUDAD BLANCA

El sol quema copos de luz
sobre los muros
y el agua repleta de sí misma
habla con furia y acusa
cruzan hilos tendidos
de una orilla a otra
sin llevar ni traer nada
columpiando el silencio
como red donde se enredan las ausencias
enhebrados los dientes feroces del amor
las palabras del amor perenne
los gestos
los cabellos

INCLEMENCY

A tree in the middle of the street
among shining cars
and dark passers-by
its harsh profile
throws out flowery speeches
to the smoke that devours them.

*   *   *   *

MOUNTAIN PATH

Over
the sheer abysm
cut from the sky
the clean drop
without rocks or vegetal obstructions
just wind crossing
through the gorge
just darkness lengthily
incubated.
On the peak
climbing over it
air forced over air
and steel foam,
fragile and bold rises
a structure of emptiness.

*   *   *   *

WHITE CITY

Sun burns flakes of light
upon the walls
and the rain, replete with itself,
speaks with fury and accusation,
extended threads cross
from one edge to another
without taking or bringing anything
swinging the silence
like a net where absences are entangled
the ferocious teeth of love strung together
words of eternal love
gestures
locks of hair

los naipes
que no aguardan
abandonados al impulso de un viento anclado
calles de espacios libres
blancas plazas marinas
muros de sol desnudo
derramándose en los vasos
los escorpiones
visitantes de la hamaca
clavan su puñal de sueño en las mejillas
más dulce que la miel
más amargo
inútil aguijón de la ternura
ciudad adánica
bullendo de ausencias
quieta en el agua dorada
sombría y quieta
escultura de sí misma
única playa
donde es posible
el encuentro de los náufragos.

*   *   *   *

Entrañable ciudad
hecha de luz y espanto
hecha de sueños
vaso dilatado
del agua que todos beben
ciega eres
pero te despliegas en lenguas
en voces de ira y de ternura
que brotan como manantiales lentos
o vomitan su desesperanza..
Ciudad hecha de aire
de ventanas que surgen entre las nubes
y puertas por las que todos y nadie pasa
hecha del color de las multitudes
levantada con los materiales de la muerte
que te ronda como fiera enjaulada.

*   *   *   *

playing cards
that won't wait
abandoned to the prompting of an anchored wind
streets with open spaces
white marinas
thick walls of naked sun
spilling into glasses
scorpions
visitors on the hammock
stick sleepy daggers into one's cheeks
sweeter than honey
more bitter
useless sting of tenderness
Adam-like city
bubbling over with absences
quiet in its golden water
dark and quiet
a sculpture of itself
the only beach
where it's possible
to encounter shipwrecked people .

*   *   *   *

Intimate city
made of light and fright
made of dreams
a dilated vessel
of the water everyone drinks
you are blind
but you display yourself in languages
in voices of ire and of love
that blossom like slow springs
or vomit their despair...
City made of air
of windows springing up among the clouds
and doors through which everyone and no one passes
made from the color of the multitudes
erected with the materials of death
that court you like a caged beast.

*   *   *   *

EL RUIDO DE LAS HOJAS

Ansiada voz
de cristal helado
voz del viento
de guitarra en llamas
susurro de hoja quebrada.

*   *   *   *

INSTANTE

Como un huevo claro
dentro del cascarón
un instante
redondo y puro
sin mancha
sin matices de tierra
sin las oscuras vetas
del pensamiento.
Un sólo instante recuperado
izado
como una uva negra
desde el fondo del vino
un instante dilatado
abierto quitasol blanco
sobre las flores rojas de la tarde.
Un canto doliente
llega en cascadas sonoras
y extiende
sus alas sobre el tiempo.
Instantáneo gozo
agua hirviente del recuerdo
instante entero
llama lenta
y voraz de la memoria.

Ciudad blanca

****

CUARTO MENGUANTE (fragmento)

En la planicie
la noche cierra el candado
latiendo al fondo

THE SOUND OF THE LEAVES

A voice longed for
of frozen crystal
voice of the wind
of the guitar in flames
whisper of a broken leaf.

*　　　　*　　　　*　　　　*

INSTANT

Like the white of an egg
inside its shell
an instant
round and pure
spotless
without traces of soil
without the dark veins
of thoughts.
One solitary instant recovered
raised high
like a dark grape
rising from the depths of wine
a delayed instant
a white parasol opened
above the red flowers of the afternoon.
A mournful song
arrives in sonorous cascades
and spreads
its wings upon time.
An instant joy
bubbling water of the memory
an entire instant
a slow and voracious
flame of memory.

Ciudad blanca

****

A QUARTER MOON WANING (fragment)

On the plains
night locks the padlock
beating inside

la puerta roja
es un reloj
de campanadas contenidas

todo se apaga
                salvo la luz
inclinada sobre el pozo
sacando cubos de agua
que la sombra devora.

Recuento del agua

****

LA PLUMA

gris
revuelo
del vuelo
del ave
lenta caída
en el estrépito
del pavimento.

Maquinaria mínima

*   *   *   *

LA PUERTA ENTREABIERTA
deja ver
y oculta
la onda que se inicia
el brillo breve anunciado en el muro.
Fluye la arena
derramándose
desde lo oscuro
aunque la puerta no es barca
y el aire es incoloro
y la angustia
algo viaja por la tormenta.

*   *   *   *

the red door
is a clock
of restrained bell strokes

everything shuts down
               except the light
inclined over the pool
extracting buckets of water
that the dark devours.

Recuento del agua

****

THE FEATHER

gray
stirring
of flight
of the bird
a slow fall
to the din
of the pavement.

Maquinaria mínima

*   *   *   *

THE DOOR AJAR
lets one see
and it hides
the wave that begins
the brief brilliance announced on the wall.
Sand flows
pouring out
from darkness
though the door is not a ship
and the air is colorless
and the anguish
something makes its way through the storm.

*   *   *   *

AMARILLA
me llama
entrelaza mis palabras
encadena
recoge uvas con la boca
y las pone en mi boca.

Me conoce
más que yo que no sé
quién soy ni para qué.

Sabia se retira
          pero ritma lo que hago
          tras la puerta.

*   *   *   *

LA CASA
              amarilla
toda ventanas sin vidrios
puro aire
ni piedra ni ladrillo ni madera
              amarilla.
sin flores
sin color en los muros
              toda amarillo
andamios
de un estar entretejido.

*   *   *

ESTA ES LA CASA
amarilla
cerrada nuez
abierta a la marea.
Lenta la luz
la construye:
paredes sólidas
verano en las ventanas
y color que asciende
          serpiente de oro
por los muros desnudos
y la ciñe.
              Casa amarilla

****

YELLOW
calls me
it entwines my words
it chains me
it gathers grapes with its mouth
and places them in my mouth.

It knows me
more than I, who doesn't know
who or why I am.

Wisely, it withdraws
            but instills rhythm in what I do
            behind the door.

*   *   *   *

THE HOUSE
                    yellow
windows everywhere without panes
pure air
not stone nor brick nor wood
                    yellow.
no flowers
no color on the walls
                    everything yellow
scaffolds
of an interwoven presence.

*   *   *   *

THIS IS THE HOUSE
yellow
a closed walnut
open to the tides.
Slowly light
constructs it:
solid walls
summer through the windows
and color that ascends
            serpent of gold
along the naked walls
and encloses it.
                    Casa amarilla

****

Desatadas las amarras
es un río de piedras el que llega
desde adentro
rodando
las piedras se agolpan
se acumulan
cierran filas
crecen
levantan la muralla
más alta
más densa
más cierta
el territorio del claustro.

*   *   *   *

En la tarde quieta
pleno el sol sobre los muros
la sombra
                su espada caída bajo el árbol
aguarda
se pondrá de pie
y se batirá sobre los muros
tajos de luz y sombra
se hundirán en la corriente
de las piedras mudas.

Los muros del claustro

****

The ties undone
it's a river of stones that comes
from inside
rolling
the stones pile up
accumulate
close ranks
grow
erect the wall
taller
denser
more definite
the territory of the cloister.

*   *   *   *

In the quiet of an afternoon
a full sun on stone walls
the shadow
            its sword fallen beneath the tree
awaits
it will get up
and will beat upon the walls
slices of light and shadow
will sink in the current
of the mute stones.

Los muros del claustro

****

9

Fernando Rosso

I, 2

Volviendo de la noche despejados de
    párpados
revoleamos los ojos sobre nuestros
    hombros errantes
los pasos entre afiladas puntas de hueso
    floridos

Limbo sedentario donde los sueños
    acaban
para encontrar la noche en las tinieblas
al azar del tiempo desteñido de imposible

*   *   *   *

I, 4

Los engendros y las imágenes
    nos pertenecen
no hay caminos ni regalos ni recorrido
nuestro único recuerdo son los amigos
muertos en días de fiesta
al repetir el contorno de las ventanas
    abiertas

El viento acompaña al agua
y un río de piedras desciende de la nieve

*   *   *   *

II, 2

Imposible hablar con nadie
se ha roto el sagrado hilo que nos une
    a las cosas
y una triste independencia nos corrompe
    sin remedio

Estamos a la par de algo que no es nuestro
seremos los perdidos de siempre
porque recorremos los senderos de la lluvia
con ojos afelpados por la sombra.

*   *   *   *

I, 2

Returning from night with
       eyelids cleared up
we flutter our eyes above our
       wandering shoulders
steps—among sharpened points of bones—
       florid

A sedentary limbo where dreams
       come to an end
to find night in the darkness
in the randomness of a time discolored with impossible

*   *   *   *

I, 4

Fetuses and images
   belong to us
there are no roads nor gifts nor trips
our only memory is of dead friends
on holidays
upon repeatng the contour of open
   windows

Wind accompanies water
and a river of stones descends from the snow.

*   *   *   *

II, 2

It's impossible to speak with anyone
the sacred thread that unites us to things
       has been broken
and a sad independence unavoidably
corrupts us

We're on equal footing with something not ours
we'll be the usual clueless ones
because we travel the paths of rain
with eyes made velvety by gloom.

*   *   *   *

116

II, 6

Sobre la sucesión de estrellas y gritos
  en la oscuridad
números vanos ahuecan la armonía
  de los signos
y los fantasmas habitan sus visiones
entre vagos vapores y amigos de regreso

A falta de palabras hablan las cosas
  todos los días
allí donde duermo y recupero mi forma
y en esa hora
que ni amarga ni perdida
será tan solamente

Algo está reservado siempre
para el que espera su silencio

El danzante y la muerte

****

8

Todo acaba
aturde esta certeza antigua
sabor de cada día

*   *   *   *

Una gota el horizonte
y vuelve la lejanía

Aire hereje

****

COPA DEL DÍA

Entre mil que vendrán
Pase mi copa este día
En su altura
La nieve cerca
El viento arma la pisada
Y la sed

II, 6

As for the succession of stars and cries
   in the darkness
vain numbers hollow out the harmony
   of signs
and ghosts inhabit their visions
among vague vapors and returning friends

With words lacking, things speak
     every day
there, where I sleep and get back in shape
and in that hour
neither bitter nor lost
will only just be

Something is always reserved
for those who wait for their silence

El danzante y la muerte

****

8

Everything comes to an end
that ancient certainty bewilders
the savoring of every day

*   *   *   *

Just a drop of horizon
and distance returns

Aire hereje

****

DRINK OF THE DAY

Among the thousand on their way
Pass me my drink on this day
In its high reaches
Snow so near
Wind readies the tread
And the thirst

118

Recuerda
La sal de la vida

*   *   *   *

COPA DE VELA

Somos el alba amigos
El duelo del cielo
Sea para cada uno
Copas y cantares

*   *   *   *

COPA DE MIEDO

La tenebrosa noche
que sin vino deja
Quien no teme, bebe
Su almohada sonámbula

*   *   *   *

COPA DE ABRA

Donde anoche
En apacheta*
Te tomamos
Para pasar las alturas.

**Bol. Lugar elevado de caminos o montañas al que
se atribuye carácter sagrado según antiguas tradiciones
indígenas.*

Copas

****

1

Esplendor de la vida
entre tanta sombra

la amistad del tiempo
repite la hora de siempre
sobre la tierra

Remember
The salt of life

*   *   *   *

DRINK FOR A VIGIL

Friends, we are the dawn
The mourning of the sky
Let each one have
Drinks and songs

*   *   *   *

A SCARY DRINK

The dark night
that leaves no wine
Those without fear, a drink:
Their somnambulist pillow

*   *   *   *

DRINK FOR A MOUNTAIN PASS

Where last night
In the apacheta*
We drank you
To get over the heights.

*Bolivia: An elevated area on roads or mountains
given a sacred significance according to ancient
indigenous traditions.

Copas

****

1

Splendor of life
among so much gloom

the friendship of time
repeats the same old hour
upon earth

Camino del río siento la arboleda
y el agua que aclara inútil
donde el sol no se detiene
ni por amor

Los días

****

2

La tarde expone el hábito inseguro
volcada en todo
pagada de su sombra

¡más paisajes y más celajes!
y ventear donde quise
el olor de los nombres
a esa hora donde surte el enigma
y aloja
sombreando el fruto

Crece el cielo lejos de la mañana
nada más en derredor
no se va la tarde
cae

*   *   *   *

3

Desaforar páginas
dejando las hojas
atrapadas o perdidas
y con cercano acento
acometer al odre cálido
dando tiempo a la vista
gesto y gasto justo

La vida cuadra
y llena de olvido todo
sólo quiere la vida
no la prueba

Tarde

****

I feel the grove on the way to the river
and the water that uselessly clears
where the sun doesn't dither
not even for love

Los días

****

2

Dusk exposes its uncertain habit
it turns over on everything,
its shadow has been paid

more landscapes and varicolored clouds!
and where I wanted, I aired out
the smell of names
at that hour when the enigma furnishes
and lodges
casting a shadow on its fruit

The sky grows, far from morning
nothing nearby
dusk doesn't leave
it falls

*   *   *   *

3

Violating pages
leaving sheets
trapped or lost
and with a close accent
undertaking a warm wineskin
taking time for the eyes,
the gesture and the right effort

Life squares up and fills
everything with forgetfulness
it only wants life
it doesn't prove it

Tarde

****

La memoria
vagabundea junto al presente
sin competir
redondea
sella el pasmo
vive todavía
sin pena ni miedo
lo que no sabemos
y lo que sabemos

El eje de las horas

****

Memory
wanders about next to the present
without competing
it rounds off
it seals off astonishment
it still relives
—without shame, without fear—
what we don't know
and what we do know

El eje de las horas

****

10

Pedro Shimose

ALBA EN LAS SOMBRAS, 14

Sometimiento humano al dolor humano.
Desde el pensamiento
las sombras profundizan su anatema en las marismas,
susurro obsceno en la hojarasca y el mantillo.
Una mujer se despierta y las primeras luces le hablan
    de los días humildes al calor del fuego.
Por las brasas una mujer avanza al encuentro del hombre

La primavera no se negó al guayabo.
El aguacero amaneció en el árbol de la goma
y un cántico descendió al principio del mundo.

Triludio en el exilio

****

AMERICAN WAY OF LIFE / BOLIVIA

Te quieren hacer de nylon,
te quieren fabricar un corazón de plástico,
te filmarán la sonrisa, te medirán el cráneo,
te vestirán de marines y bases militares,
codificarán tu amor para sus computadoras,
te desnudarán en sínodos sangrientos,
te harán bailar cuando les dé la gana,
strip-tease for Hollywood, American Dream
    Corporation,
cantarás huaynos para "La Voz de América"
y contarás tu vida en el *Reader's Digest.*

Fabricarán tus sueños en colores,
te darán sortilegios en conserva,
pop in out camp very good Batman yes!
reducción india para un *week-end Made in USA*
Visión publicará un reportaje con afiches de turismo,
te instalarán escaleras mecánicas de bajada
                (nunca de subida)
enviciarán tu aire, tu cielo azul sera un túmulo oscuro
y dirán *BOLIVIA TYPICAL COUNTRY IT'S WONDERFUL*
crecerán rascacielos, te encerrarán en jaulas,
te enseñarán cómo se caza el dólar,
                programarán tu alma
y tomarás píldoras para dormir. . .
*   *   *   *

DAWN IN THE SHADOWS, 14

Human submission to human sorrow.
Originating from thought
shadows fathom their anathema in the salt marshes,
an obscene murmur in the fallen leaves and the humus.
A woman awakens and the first lights speak to her
       of the humble days in the fire's heat.
Through burning coals the woman advances to meet the man

The spring didn't deny itself to the guava tree
The morning shower appeared upon the rubber tree
and a canticle descended upon the beginning of the world.

                      Triludio en el exilio

****

AMERICAN WAY OF LIFE / BOLIVIA

They want to make you out of nylon,
they want to manufacture a plastic heart for you,
they will film your smile, measure your cranium,
they'll dress you with marines and military bases,
they'll codify your love for their computers,
they'll undress you in bloody synods,
they'll make you dance whenever they please,
strip-tease for Hollywood, American Dream
    Corporation,
you'll sing Andean songs for "The Voice of America"
and you'll tell your life story in *Reader's Digest.*

They'll manufacture your dreams in colors,
they'll give you canned sorceries,
pop in out camp very good Batman yes!
an Indian reservation for a *Made-in-U.S.A. weekend*
Visión magazine will publish a report with travel posters
they'll install down-only escalators (never up-only)
they'll foul your air, your blue sky will be a dark tumulus
and they'll say *BOLIVIA TYPICAL COUNTRY*
                     IT'S WONDERFUL
skyscrapers will grow, they'll lock you up in cages,
they'll teach you how to hunt the dollar,
                 they'll program your soul
and you'll take sleeping pills. . .
*   *   *   *

EPIGRAMA PEQUEÑOBURGUÉS SUPERACADÉMICORREALISTA

Después de impresionar a las muchachas con nuestro
        ingenio;
después de violar vestales y de escandalizar monjas;
después de quemar lirios, enterrar nubes e incendiar
        templos;
después de degollar vacas sagradas y asesinar dioses;
después de escribir sin mayúsculas y sin signos de
        puntuación;
después de atacar a la rosa y al rey Gustavo de Suecia;
después de dinamitar museos y bailar en los
        cementerios,
de perseguir la gloria y soñar que nos acostamos
        con ella;
después de pelear con dragones, imperios y quimeras,
de gemir porque publiquen nuestro nombre en los
        periódicos
y de reunirnos por la madrugada para derribar
        pirámides,
¿qué nos queda?

un sillón en la academia
y una chequera.
        Quiero escribir pero me sale espuma

****

DIÁLOGO EN PIEDRA, VI

Mareas de hombres ciegos y desnudos
vagan
        errantes
por la negra espesura de tus símbolos
y no eres capaz de descifrar silencios,
tierra enferma de arrogancia.

*   *   *   *

TIWANAKU*

Tu nombre amarillea,
                oscurece y
                        cae,
gastado,

A PETTY-BOURGEOIS
SUPERACADEMICREALIST

After impressing the girls with our
        ingeniousness;
after raping vestals and scandalizing nuns;
after burning irises, burying clouds and igniting
        temples;
after sacrificing sacred cows and assassinating gods;
after writing without capital letters and without
        punctuation marks;
after attacking the rose and King Gustave of Sweden;
after dynamiting museums and dancing in the
        cemeteries,
pursuing glory and dreaming of going to bed
        with her;
after battling dragons, empires, and chimeras,
groaning because they might publish our name in
        newspapers
and getting together at daybreak to knock down
        pyramids,
what's left for us?

a seat in the academy
and a checkbook.
        Quiero escribir pero me sale espuma

****

DIALOGUE IN STONE, VI

Tides of blind, naked men
roam about
        wandering
through the black thicket of your symbols
and you're not able to decipher silences,
sick land of arrogance.

*   *   *   *

TIWANAKU*

Your name turns yellow,
           darkens and
                    falls,
worn thin,

al fondo de la piedra.
                        Todo es muerte en ti,
figuración del tiempo,
                        muerte que no acaba
          de morir,
                        muerte en lucha a muerte
con tus dioses
                        y tus ángeles de piedra.
          Profundo,
                    el sueño de la piedra
intenta definirte
pero el frío
          se filtra por tus ojos,
                    se hace noche en ti,
          tristeas,
      tus siglos son escombros,
tu sombra
se derrumba
          a cada instante,
se agrieta
              a cada instante,
se desploma en el polvo
          a cada instante.
                        Tu funeral
camina
          por telarañas y tormentas.
                    El olor de la muerte
                    te persigue:
tu escarcha envejecida,
          tu paciencia arrugada,
                    tu círculo,
                    tus sellos.
Ya no estás,
                    piedra vencida, ciega,
piedra de soledad,
                    te estás muriendo,
piedra demolida,
                    de la noche a la noche,
                    tu nombre es nada,
piedra sometida,
piedra de silencio,
piedra.

* Tiwanaku: sitio arqueológico pre-colombino.

*   *   *   *

at the bottom of the stone.
                         All within you is death,
a representation of time,
                         death that hasn't
           just died,
                         death in a fight to the end
with your gods
                         and your angels of stone.
           Profound,
                         the dream of the stone
attempts to define you
but the cold
           filters through your eyes,
                         inside you it becomes night,
           you become sad,
      your centuries are rubble,
your shadow
crumbles
           every moment,
cracks
           every moment,
it topples in the dust
           every moment.
                         Your funeral
advances
           through spider webs and storms.
                         The smell of death
                         pursues you:
your aged frost,
           your withered patience,
                your circle,
                your graven seals.
You are no longer here,
                blind, defeated stone,
stone of solitude,
                         you are dying,
demolished stone,
                overnight
                your name means nothing,
subdued stone,
stone of silence,
stone.

*Tiwanaku: pre-Colombian archeological site.

*   *   *   *

POSIBLE IMPOSIBLE

> *Ante una araña encapsulada en ámbar*
> *hace 52.875.000 años*

Tal vez un cuarzo o un pedazo de granito
sorprendan con el rayo un día
    a una mujer sentada
    o a un hombre de rodillas;

quizás un cristal o un alabastro
guarden la forma pura
de la llama
        y el vuelo
            de la chispa,
pero
¿cómo eternizar la cólera del fuego?
           ¿la ternura del fuego?
         ¿la palabra del fuego?

Tal vez una moneda
        o un grano de mostaza
repitan pájaros y sueños
            cuando nadie
recuerde la cualidad del lirio y el
atributo de la
ola.

        Caducidad del fuego

****

TIMONEL DE LOS VIENTOS, II

> *A J.F.K.*

Has crecido de repente con un tiro en la cabeza.
Dolorosa,
    tu sangre corrió de casa en casa
en forma de noticia.
        Anochecido en la grandeza
te marchas
por el lento redoble de tambores sobre la verde
      llanura de Arlington,
        El Potomac
      sigue fluyendo, Capitán, oh Capitán,
    y tú

POSSIBLE IMPOSSIBLE

In the presence of a spider capsuled
in amber 52,875,000 years ago

Perhaps a piece of quartz or granite
will someday catch a sitting woman
     or a kneeling man
     with a bolt of lightning;

maybe a piece of crystal or alabaster
will retain the pure form
of a flame
     and the flight
          of a spark,
but
how to eternalize the anger of fire?
     the tenderness of fire?
     the language of fire?

Perhaps a coin
     or a mustard seed
will repeat birds and dreams
        when no one
will remember the qualities of the iris and the
attributes of the
wave.

               Caducidad del fuego

****

HELMSMAN OF THE WINDS, II

To J.F.K.

You have suddenly grown with a bullet in your head.
Painfully,
     your blood ran from house to house
taking form as news.
         Night has fallen on greatness
you leave
with the slow roll of the drums upon the green
       plains of Arlington,
        The Potomac
     goes flowing on, Captain, oh Captain
     and you

penetras en las aguas profundas
de la Historia, con tu sonrisa
triste.

Al pie de la letra

****

INTRODUCCIÓN A LA COSA

Este poema
forma parte de un libro del cual se tirarán
500 ejemplares.

De esos 500 ejemplares
se regalarán 50,

de los cuales
se leerán 5,

de los cuales
sólo 1
será comprendido.

Vale la pena.

Reflexiones maquiavélicas

****

HUELGA DE HAMBRE

—Mi palabra es estaño, pero no vale nada.
—Nadie me hace caso.
—Mi palabra es pobre y no se escucha.

—Mi hombre no está contra el gobierno
    pero tenemos hambre—diciendo,
decía una mujer con su guagüita en brazos.

La ciudad
no sabe lo que pasa más allá de
la ciudad.
        Usted, por ejemplo, huiracocha,
vive preocupado si su mujercita le pone cuernos,
si su gastritis,
si su reuma. . .

fathom the deep waters
of History, with your sad
smile.

Al pie de la letra

****

INTRODUCTION TO THE THING

This poem
forms part of a book of which 500 copies
will be printed.

Of those 500 copies
50 will be gifts,

of which
5 will be read,

of which
only 1
will be understood.

It's worth it.

Reflexiones maquiavélicas

****

HUNGER STRIKE

"My word is of tin, but it's not worth anything."
"Nobody pays attention to me."
"My words are poor and not heard."

"My husband is not against the government
  but we're hungry," she was saying,
a woman was saying with her baby in her arms.

The city
doesn't know what's happening beyond
the city.
    You, for example, sir, spend your life worrying
            if your little woman is unfaithful,
if your gastritis,
if your rheumatism. . .

así es la ciudad nomás pues
con su bulla y sus prisas;
así es el mundo: lleno de problemas
y estamos cansados de verle la cara al hambre
todos los días hasta en sueños,
de toparnos con sus fusiles
apuntándonos más de cuatro siglos.

Ya no tenemos miedo, huiracocha*.   [*caballero]
Por eso hemos venido
a denunciar con hambre nuestra hambre.
Y si el gobierno se digna escuchar nuestra
palabra,
sin balearnos,
créame, patroncito, que igual nomás
nuestros días seguirán siendo largos
y tristes
como muchos días de hambre:
nuestra vida,
nuestra historia. . .

*   *   *   *

COMO EL FUEGO

A Jaime Choque

Ya no sentimos vergüenza de salir a la calle y
codearnos con el mundo.

Aquí están el sudor y la sangre—nuestra sangre
el dolor y la tierra—nuestra tierra

(Miro lo mío—lo que siempre fue mío)

Ahora nuestros corazones arden como el fuego
y nuestros pensamientos son relámpagos.

Como llamas
nuestros padres fueron arreados a la guerra.
Carne de cañón, morían
sin saber por qué
—simplemente servían de escalera—
nuestros padres
fueron enterrados
vivos

that's just the way the city is, you know
with its hustle and bustle;
that's the way the world is: full of problems
and we're tired of staring hunger in the face
every day, even in dreams,
of running up against their firearms
pointing at us for over four centuries.

We're no longer afraid, sir.
That's why we've come
to denounce our hunger with hunger.
And if the government deigns to listen to our
words,
without shooting us,
believe me, boss, that our days like always
will just go on being long
and sad
like many days of hunger:
our life,
our history. . .

*   *   *   *

LIKE FIRE

For Jaime Choque

We no longer feel shame going out on the street
and jostling the world.

Here they are, blood and sweat—our blood
and pain and our land—our land

(I look at what's mine—what's always been mine)

Now our hearts are burning like fire
and our thoughts are flashes of lightening.

Like flames
our fathers were herded away to war.
Cannon fodder, they died
without knowing why
—they simply served as a ladder—
our fathers
were buried
alive

en la mina;
nos trataban como a bestias
—"indio bruto", diciendo, nos reñían
como a niños malcriados—
ni una camisa de tocuyo siquiera podíamos vestir,
nos prohibían entrar en las ciudades,
—"pongos con taquia"—nos vendían
y nadie protestaba
para sufrir miseria estábamos,
a empellones,
para sufrir desprecios,
para eso estábamos. . .

Nos quitaron la tierra,
nos embrutecieron,
                    pero ya no sentimos miedo
(nunca más volveremos a sentir miedo, te juro)
ya hemos aprendido a hablar tu lengua, huiracocha,
para decirte que somos hombres—muchos hombres—
y que nuestros corazones
arden como el mismísimo fuego.

*   *   *   *

ESCRITO EN EL LAGO TUMICHUCUA

a Rosarillo

A 10.000 kms. de ti, descubro
a un hombre
acostumbrado a otro país,
a otra ciudad,
            a otras amistades.
Mi país:
        humo de nostalgia,
casi un sueño.
            Cuando recorro
estos caminos polvorientos
te siento pegadita a mí,
con tu risa llenándolo todo,
amando lo que yo amo, naturalmente,
doliéndote conmigo en esta pena
difícil y profunda,
                    ¡yo qué sé!

Mi madre y mis amigos me han traído

in the mine;
they treated us like animals
             —saying, "dumb Indian," they scolded us
like ill-bred children—
we couldn't even wear a coarse cotton shirt,
they wouldn't let us enter cities,
—"filthy servants "—they sold us
and no one protested
we were meant to suffer in misery,
shoved around,
to suffer contempt,
that's what we were there for. . .

They took away our land,
they stupefied us,
             but we no longer feel fear
(never again will we return to feel it, I swear)
now we've learned to speak your language, sir,
to tell you we are men—many men—
and that our hearts
burn with the very same fire.

*   *   *   *

WRITTEN ON LAKE TUMICHUCUA

To Rosarillo

10,000 kms. from you, I discover
a man
accustomed to another country,
to another city,
             to other friends.
My country:
             smoke of nostalgia,
almost a dream.
             When I go down
these dusty roads
I feel you right up close to me,
with your laughter filling everything,
loving what I love, naturally,
and hurting with me in this difficult
and profound grief,
             what do I know?

My mother and my friends have brought me

140

al lago.
        A ti te echo de menos
con una flor de suchi en el pelo prendida
como cuando estábamos juntos
aquí,
        bajo las palmeras,
en el agua tibia y clara de la felicidad,
cosechando lunas
bajo los floridos toborochis
de nuestra juventud.

Pero no estás junto a mí
y yo tampoco estoy conmigo.
Más triste sin ti es la tristeza de amar
a este país. Sólo espero
volver a verte pronto,
antes de que el tiempo
nos borre y llegue
la época de lluvias.

                    Bolero de caballería

****

BANQUETE

Joyas lucientes,
trajes escotados,
manos educadas
para sostener
cubiertos de oro y plata.

Espérame a los postres
sin ligueros ni tules,
con sólo dos gotitas
de perfume en el cuello,
dispuesta a explicarme
por qué nuestras miradas
se cruzaron.

*   *   *   *

CÓPULA

Vaciarme en ti.
Morir dentro de ti
para nacerme

to the lake.
　　　　I miss you
with a suchi flower pinned to your hair
like when we were together
here,
　　　　under the palm trees,
in the clear, warm water of happiness,
harvesting moons
beneath the toborochi trees
of our youth.

But you are not at my side
and neither am I with myself.
Even sadder than being without you is the sadness
of loving this country. I only hope
to return to see you soon,
before time
erases us and
the rainy season arrives.
　　　　　　　　　　Bolero de caballería

****

BANQUET

Glittering jewels
well-fitted suits,
hands educated
to hold
dinnerware of gold and silver.

Wait for me afterwards,
without garters or tulle,
with only two little drops
of perfume on your neck,
ready to explain to me
why we exchanged
glances.

*　　　　　*　　　　　*　　　　　*

COPULATION

Emptying myself into you.
Dying within you
to be born

142

en vivo fuego, ardiendo.

En ti me crezco entero,
con tal querer
que me dejo morir
en tu carne mortal
sacudida
por este cataclismo.

*   *   *   *

LA MUSA SE VA

No me has visto sonarme las narices,
toser;
ir al baño, tirar de la cadena.
No has olido el humo en mis cabellos
cuando llego del trabajo;

no has besado la sal de mi cansancio,
ni me has visto poniéndome el pijama,
ni me has oído roncar a pierna suelta,
ni has soportado mis cabreos
al amanecer,
cuando se corta la ducha y estoy enjabonado.

La verdad está en la gripe
y la ropa sudada;

en el olor a huevo frito,
a ollas y sartenes sucias;
en los discos de boleros
rayados por el uso;

en los minutos fatales
que siguen al choque de los cuerpos
(cuando pides un klínex
o enciendes un cigarro);
en la cara de los protagonistas
que ya no ríen cuando se cuentan chistes
porque la noche avanza
y el tiempo no perdona.

No te lo vas a creer

****

in a bright fire, burning.

Within you I become myself,
with such a wanting
that I let myself die
in your mortal flesh
so shaken
by this cataclysm.

*   *   *   *

THE MUSE DEPARTS

You haven't seen me blow my nose,
and cough;
go to the bathroom, pull the chain.
You haven't smelled the smoke in my hair
when I arrive from work;

you haven't kissed the salt of my fatigue,
nor have you seen me slip into my pajamas,
nor have you heard me snore the roof off,
nor have you put up with my tantrums,
at dawn,
when the shower stops and I'm all lathered up.

The truth is in the flu
and the sweaty clothes;

in the smell of fried eggs,
of dirty pots and pans;
in the bolero records
scratched by use;

in the fatal minutes
that follow the clash of bodies
(when you ask for a Kleenex
or light a cigarette);
on the face of the protagonists
who no longer laugh at jokes
because night advances
and time offers no pardon.

No te lo vas a creer

****

FAX NADA URGENTE

Después de tres cafés
me sobran las alquimias.
Curado del estrés,
supero lipotimias.

Mis dolencias, ya ves,
son afecciones nimias.
Males de la vejez:
insomnios y bulimias.

El sístole aburrido
y el diástole cansado
repiten el maullido

de un gato enamorado.
(Largo y hondo quejido
de un macho engatusado).

Riberalta y otros poemas

****

A NOT-SO-URGENT FAX

After three coffees
I have too many alchemies.
Free from stress,
I overcome fainting spells.

My ailments, you see,
are trivial conditions.
Elderly afflictions:
insomnia and bulimia.

The bored systole
and the tired diastole
repeat the mewing

of an enamored cat.
(A long and deep lament
of a macho who's been tricked.)

Riberalta y otros poemas

****

11

Vilma Tapia

Las mañanas de septiembre son
por el lila jacarandá
velo de bodas de jóvenes horas
unidas a techos de tejas
en pasteles

Del deseo y la rosa

*   *   *   *

No faltará quien al pasar
se detenga

Con la cara pegada a las rejas
atento
escuchará los cantos
reconocerá los matices
de los plumajes
y hasta el más leve
temblor de las alas

Entonces podrás abrir la puerta
permitir que se pasee
por tu jardín
enseñarle dos o tres modos
de aproximarse a tus pájaros
de cuidar de ellos
de alimentarlos.

Corazones de terca escama

****

Sumergidas en tiempos ajenos
enamoradas y anhelantes
como caracolas en la orilla
repetimos el mar.
Nuestros ojos miran por otros:
toda piel humana es nuestra.
Inconsolables por la pérdida
bebemos lo invisible.

*   *   *   *

Una en mí quiere alcanzarme
devolverme.
Me quiere hilo de la urdimbre.

Mornings in September
are because of the violet jacaranda
a bridal veil at weddings of young people,
hours together under tile roofs,
pastries

Del deseo y la rosa

****

There's always someone who
stops when passing

With his face stuck in the grating
attentive
who will listen to the songs
and will recognize the nuances
of the plumage
and even the slightest
tremor of the wings

Then you can open the door
letting him stroll
through your garden
showing him two or three ways
to approach your birds
to care for them
to feed them.

Corazones de tercera escama

****

Submerged in other times
enamored and desirous
like snails on the edge
we repeat the sea.
Our eyes search for others:
all human flesh is ours.
Inconsolable for the loss
we drink what is invisible.

*   *   *   *

One inside of me wants to catch me
send me back.
She wants me for a warping thread.

Quiere que reconozca la tierra que piso
que encuentre en mí el grito
que me adhiera a una bandera.

Pero en mí nada empieza, ni se agota
nada me contiene, nada contengo

¿Y mis raíces?
desatadas
—ya pájaros—
andan sueltas.

*   *   *   *

En pos de ti
he ido por mil direcciones
ninguna equivocada.

A mi madre

****

De alguna manera
el viento fue enemigo tuyo
el viento dañaba tu piel
no te aveniste con él.
Y este aquí es viento
es frío, soledad y miseria.

Poco a poco buscaste estar muerta
y eres tan hermosa dormida
                    intacta
                    reconciliada con el cuerpo.

¿Desde cuándo quisiste estar muerta?
¿Lo quisiste de veras?

Te veía ir y venir
sin saber en qué orilla anclar
ciega a las luciérnagas
empujabas el silencio con tus remos.

Herida, tu combate resultaba amargo
El dolor mordió tu belleza
mientras estabas viva.
¿Se puede comprender eso?

She wants me to recognize the land I tread
to find within me the cry
that might bind me to a flag.

But nothing in me begins, nor tires
nothing contains me, I contain nothing

And my roots?
untied
—like birds—
they go about free.

*   *   *   *

Pursuing you
I've gone off in a thousand directions
none mistaken.

A mi madre

****

Somehow
the wind was your enemy
the wind damaged your skin
you disagreed with it.
And this here is wind
it is cold, solitary and miserable.

Little by little, you sought death
and you are so beautiful asleep
                    intact
                    reconciled with your body.

How long have you wished to be dead?
Did you really wish it?

I saw you come and go
not knowing on which shore to anchor,
blind to the fireflies,
you pushed silence with your oars.

Once hurt, your combat ended bitterly
Pain bit into your beauty
while you were alive.
Does that make sense?

Pero te alzas
en tus gestos puros y brillantes.
Hoy noche te tenemos de regreso
la lámpara de la infancia
alumbra tu imagen blanca, casi transparente.
Eres paz y promesa
vuelves bañada por las estrellas.
Con tus manos extendidas y toda tu fuerza
vences los opacos límites
para acariciar tu sangre.

Él te ofrece su mejilla
él te pide consuelo.

Se hará el jardín que querías
y tus gestos abrirán las sendas
y serán la lluvia.
Estaremos contigo
en tus ojos, en esas aguas de hermoso color
y en tus manos
que al fin sueltan el frío.

*　　　　*　　　　*　　　　*

Mientras el cielo se prepara para una luna llena
en mi oído se enciende un cortejo de blancas voces.

Entre las nubes, imágenes
que en mi lengua no tienen nombre
anuncian (apenas) el brillo
esparciendo por el jardín su aliento calmoso y frío.

La noche pone un aro de color a su largo dedo
y acaricia mudeces y señales cobijadas por la vida.

*　　　　*　　　　*　　　　*

Con los ojos húmedos
ansiosa
suplicante
se acomoda en mí
y espera y sonríe y otorga.

Desconfiada, desde mí
la observo:
sé que la sostendré

But you rebel
with your pure and brilliant gestures.
Tonight we have you back
the lamp of infancy lights your
white, almost transparent image.
You are peace and a promise,
you return, bathed by the stars.
With your hands held out and all your strength
you overcome opaque boundaries
to soothe your blood.

He offers you his cheek
he begs your solace.

The garden you wanted will be made
and your efforts will open paths
and they will become rain.
We will be with you, in your eyes,
in those beautifully colored tears
and in your hands,
that will finally shake off the cold.

*   *   *   *

While the sky prepares for a full moon
in my ear a train of white voices lights up.

Among the clouds, images
that on my tongue have no names
announce (hardly) a brilliance, scattering
its cold, calming breath about the garden.

Night places a colored ring on its long finger
and caresses muteness and signs covered by life.

*   *   *   *

With moist eyes
anxious
beseeching
it settles down in me
and waits and smiles and gives.

Suspicious, from within me,
I observe it
I know I'll sustain it

hasta que me incorpore y caiga
despeñada
a un costado de mi sombra.

*   *   *   *

Olvida cada letra
de mi nombre

¿No ves? su única falta
es ahogarse en el recuerdo.

¿Habrá acaso alguna voz de santo
que lo pronuncie?

*   *   *   *

Voy a cortar
del lenguaje de mi memoria
uno a uno
todos los poemas de amor
para ofrecértelos

y que florezcan
y que nos cobijen.

Oh estaciones, oh castillos

****

Cae la tarde
pastor

tu morada aguarda
en el regazo de la noche.

Luciérnagas del fondo

****

La trapecista
se sonríe
(el que la asistirá
en su muerte
percibe
su aliento)

until I sit up and fall
thrown down
alongside my shadow.

*   *   *   *

Forget every letter
of my name

Don't you see? Its only mistake
is drowning in the memory.

Can there possibly be some saintly voice
that will utter it?

*   *   *   *

I'm going to sever
from the language of my memory
one by one
all the love poems
to offer them to you

so that they will flower
and shelter us.

Oh estaciones, oh castillos

****

The afternoon darkens
shepherd

your abode awaits
in the lap of night.

Luciérnagas del fondo

****

The trapeze artist
smiles
(the one who will attend her
in her death
perceives
her breath)

una vez más
se cuelga
de un solo pie

badajo iluminado

roza de ambos los días
recoge las más tiernas fresas

y se canta

      tañe

se ciñe el cinturón
del deseo
aprieta
el gesto inmediato

los escenarios para el mañana
se mueven

Y es tu voz
la que hace rodar
mi nombre
por mi columna

*   *   *   *

5

Ovejas paseaban entre las tumbas
niña
pregunté por la virginidad
y mi himen se contrajo
tuve miedo

¿Con qué actos no se honra
a la familia?
¿Dónde se guardan los velos?
¿Será la sangre?

Cae la música de panderetas
caen las rosas
esta es la fiesta de mi boda

¿Qué pulcritud sostiene mi espalda?

once again
she hangs
by just one foot

an illuminated clapper

skims the days of them both
gathers the most tender berries

and it sings

        it tolls

she fastens her belt
of desire
tightens
her next grimace

the settings for tomorrow
are moved

And it's your voice
that makes my name
roll
down my spine.

*   *   *   *

5

Sheep passed among the tombs
little girl
I asked about virginity
and my hymen contracted
I was afraid

With what actions is the family
not honored?
Where are the veils kept?
Can it be the blood?

Music falls from the tambourines
roses fall
this is the party of my wedding

What propriety sustains my back?

La ley de Dios me acompaña

Tengo cintura de oro
lentejuelas adornan mis párpados

Mis brazos desnudos no alcanzan
esas lejanas preguntas

Sobre el palanquín
soy llevada hasta una puerta
no puedo abrirla

Padre
dime que me amas

La fiesta de mi boda

****

God's law accompanies me

I have a golden waist
glitter adorns my eyes

My bared arms can't reach
those distant questions

On a litter
I am carried to a door
I can't open it

Father
tell me you love me

La fiesta de mi boda

****

12

Antonio Terán Cabero

XX

En esta inútil geometría
de huesos
tan pronto envejecidos sin motivo,
tan livianos al tacto y a la sangre,
yo soy el que camina recogiendo
su cuerpo por la acera.

Reteniendo la tarde y sus campanas
con prestada sonrisa,
yo soy el trino,
el ala que se arruga,
ese gemido saltarín y urbano
que coge mis solapas
y precede mi sueño.

Nada tengo que hacer en esta absurda
vitrina de relojes.

Camino solamente
y recojo mi cuerpo.

De pronto se me adhiere
un lejano recuerdo de trenes olvidados,
el cartel de los pájaros
anunciando tu nombre al mediodía,
la tristeza que amaste,
tu sonrisa,
tus pasos. . .

En la torre del polvo
llama el sueño.

Soy entonces la flecha
retornando en el tiempo.

Gastado traje y lírica memoria,
alma que grita al eco,
mundo solo
y extraño.

Puerto imposible

****

XX

In this useless geometry
of bones
aged so soon for no reason,
so light to the touch and to the blood,
I'm the one who walks along collecting
its body on the sidewalk.

Retaining the evening and its bells
with a borrowed smile,
I am the triune,
the wing that wrinkles,
that restless, urban groan
that grabs my lapels
and precedes my dream.

I have nothing to do in this absurd
showcase of watches.

I just walk along
and collect my body.

Suddenly a distant memory
of forgotten trains sticks with me,
the poster of birds
announcing your name at noon,
the sadness you loved,
your smile
your steps. . .

In the tower of dust
sleep calls.

Then I'm the arrow
going back in time.

A worn suit and a lyrical memory,
a soul that shouts to an echo,
a strange and
solitary world.

Puerto imposible

****

CÓNYUGES

viejas espadas del rencor doméstico
se afilan en la sombra

desenvuelve sus crótalos el viento
y ya empuja la puerta

*   *   *   *

IV

porque hay un sitio en la tierra
donde llora su cuerpo
un eslabón sediento

una tiniebla

es la tierra que soy
y el sitio exacto en que la sueño

Y negarse a morir

****

VI

los fuegos estelares
                      leños
del amor
                  ardidos bajo el cielo de junio

la luz que nunca vino

tu voz en el florero que alumbra todavía

suave lámpara el poema
del ceibo que acabo de plantar
como quien puebla el mundo con secretas imágenes.

Bajo el ala del sombrero

****

SPOUSES

old swords of domestic rancor
are sharpened in the shadow

the wind unwraps its castanets
and now pushes the door

*   *   *   *

IV

because there's a place on earth
where its body cries
a silky link

a darkness

it's the earth that I am
and the exact place in which I dream it

Y negarse a morir

****

VI

the starry fires
                logs
of love
                burning under a June sky

the light that never came

your voice in the vase that still illuminates

a soft light, the poem
of the ceibo I've just planted,
like the one who populates the world
with secret images.

Bajo el ala del sombrero

****

FERVOR DE UN INSTANTE

abro mi puerta a tu arboleda

surtidor de esmeraldas
como la leche de mi madre

dulce lengua sonora
refugiada en mi frente

en un vuelo de hondura
me descubro tu nuevo domicilio

y así es apenas topográfica
tu muerte irremediable

*   *   *   *

ESTE AMOROSO OFICIO

y las plurales alabanzas
con que mi madre en el batán oraba

melodiosa la *llajua**
en el altar de piedra

incienso los aromas

salvaje y pura la mañana

el fervor de un instante
en la belleza de los signos

por fin la brujería de la luz
bien al fondo de las cosas

y este amoroso oficio que ahora zurce
harapo con harapo
lo que el supino dios ha dispersado.

** llajua: una salsa picante boliviana preparada
básicamente con 'locotos'(un ají boliviano)*

Ahora que es entonces

****

FERVOR OF AN INSTANT

I open my door to the woods

a supplier of emeralds
like the milk of my mother

sweet, sonorous tongue
sheltered on my face

in a flight deep down
I discover your new home

and so your inevitable death
is hardly topographical

*   *   *   *

THIS LOVING OCCUPATION

and the numerous praises with which
my mother prayed in the mill

the melodic *llajua**
on the stone altar

incense aromas

the morning savage and pure

the fervor of an instant
in the beauty of the signs

at last the sorcery of light
well into the depth of things

and this loving occupation that darns
rag with rag
all that a supine god has dispersed.

**llajua: a spicy Bolivian sauce prepared basically
with "locotos" (a Bolivian hot pepper)*

Ahora que es entonces

****

168

oh dios llévatela tienes derecho
a desandar el mundo que le diste
no hagas sucia su muerte ni hagas triste
su tránsito del limo hasta tu pecho

está sola y con miedo está deshecho
el orgullo que fue si tú pariste
su camino tan largo y permitiste
que su luz perfumara tu barbecho

deja al menos que duerma y se disuelva
en su propio perfume y que despierte
en el eterno pulso de la selva

en su cuerpo en reposo quiero verte
y viéndote quizá así te absuelva
de tanta iniquidad y tanta muerte

De aquel umbral sediento

****

CUARTETO

tu cadera mujer tibia en mi mano
respira como un sándalo infinito
teje en mi sangre símbolos del mito
y canta en mí como un profundo piano

*   *   *   *

III

Con la tiniebla cambia el mundo
viene el céfiro y clama por su antigua labranza
viene el agua y se esconde en las palabras
la transparencia muda
un torbellino
en el polvo nos borra y en el tiempo.

*   *   *   *

BOCA ABAJO Y MURCIÉLAGO

apenas un vaso como todos deshabitándose la memoria del
agua que se ausenta poco a poco del cuerpo el anticipo

oh god take her away, you have the right
to undo the world that you gave her
don't vilify her death, don't sadden her
passage from the mire into your light

alone and afraid, her pride of yesteryear
is now broken if you gave birth
to her long road and let her worth
perfume your fallow land so dear

at least let her sleep and dissolve
in her own perfume and awake
in the eternal pulse of the forest

I want to see your presence in her body in repose
and seeing you perhaps then I'll absolve
you of so much iniquity, so much death

De aquel umbral sediento

*   *   *   *

QUARTET

your hip, woman, warm upon my knee
like an infinite sandalwood it breathes,
in my blood mythical symbols it weaves
and like a deep piano, it sings within me

*   *   *   *

III

In the darkness the world changes
the zephyr comes and clamors for its old labor
the rain comes and hides within words
transparency changes
a whirlwind
erases time and us in the dust

*   *   *   *

FACE DOWN AND A BAT

hardly a glass like all of them disabling the memory of
the water takes leave little by little from the body the

de un trizado cristal y el pulso de cada día imantado al
impecable viento de popa
nada en verdad que desespere ni la prisma insensata ni el
pensamiento aciago en esta hora de certezas serenamente
bienvenidas

lo irremediable apaciguado por la antigua costumbre de
imaginar que nuestros pasos son de otro

que recordar es inventar la mayor parte
que la luz en la frente es una estrella muerta hace ya
mucho tiempo

y que así la noche se preludie con grillos agoreros no por
eso los ojos dejarán de posarse ávidamente sobre el mundo

detrás de la próxima colina aquel lugar visible siempre a
través de todas las colinas porque habita en el ser y en
lo que somos después de no haber sido
porque habita también en ese otoño de los huesos y en el
río que mojó de plegarias los senos de la madre y en el terror
sin límites cuando padre abjuró de sí mismo llenándose de
arrugas y de bondad a toda prueba

y a qué presencias tales si esta página quería solamente
proferir un tranquilo abandono y llamarle pan al pan y al
vino vino

y con menos palabras el otoño llamarse primavera

luego mano lengua silencio lo que fueras busca pronto una
puerta para huir de tanta vida tumultuosa y escribe tú una
tabla antes del naufragio

escribe finalmente que no vale la pena por ahora excavar
más allá de nuestros pies cansados

y déjanos dormir en un poema sin mayores tormentos
cada quien en su cueva boca abajo y murciélago

tapiados ciegos libres por un momento de nosotros y de
tantas metáforas.

Boca abajo y murciélago
—otras palabras al acecho—

****

foretaste of a shattered crystal and the pulse of each
day drawn to the impeccable tail wind
nothing really that despairs not the senseless prism nor
the black thought in this hour of certainties serenely
welcome

what is irremediable is soothed by the ancient custom
of imagining that our steps are of another

that remembering is mostly inventing

that light on one's face is a star, dead from long ago

and that this way the night is preceded by prescient crickets
that's not why eyes will stop posing avidly upon the world

behind the next hill that place is always visible across all the
hills because it inhabits one's being and what we are after
not having been because it also inhabits that autumn of the
bones and in the river that soaked with prayers the breasts of
the mother and in the unlimited terror when the father
renounced himself becoming filled with wrinkles
and unyielding goodness

and what presences if this page only wanted to hurl
a quiet abandonment and to call things by their name

and with less words autumn to be named spring

later hand tongue silence whatever you were quickly searches for
a door to flee from such a tumultuous life and you write
a table before the shipwreck

write finally that for now it's not worth excavating
beyond our tired feet

and let us sleep on a poem without further torment
each one in his cave face down and a bat

walled-in blind free for a moment of ourselves and of
so many metaphors.

Boca abajo y murciélago
—otras palabras al acecho—

****

13

Mónica Velásquez

SIETE MANERAS PARA DECIR EL DOLOR
POSIBILIDAD 2

Quiero hacerte una niña pequeñita
perdida de la mano de su madre,
niña guardada sin nombre
tímida y solitaria entre la maleza de las burlas
confundida miedosa ante las disciplinas
para que sepas y hurgues el desamparo
toques la nada con ambos pies, te confundas
tengas pretextos para hallar guaridas
y veas la lluvia, por fin, desde la ventana.

El viento de los náufragos

****

Descalza para no despertarte
obedeces tu profecía de pirámide
alma intocada
cuerpo sin magia
letras ajenas que soy yo—preguntas
y por primera vez, dudas

*   *   *   *

persigo tu olor
como a una palabra que duele
como al frío y mis ojeras
inundándome
ya todo el aire es tu olor
asfixiada de ti me abro
en mi boca
paralíticas
las letras de tu nombre

*   *   *   *

sin permanencia
sin hijo desde tu sábana
la muerte que te llama
te llevará intocada

*   *   *   *

SEVEN WAYS TO EXPRESS PAIN
POSSIBILITY 2

I want to make you a little girl
who strayed from her mother's hand
a girl kept without a name
timid and solitary in the weed patch of scorn
confused afraid facing punishment
so you will know and be poked by helplessness
so, with both feet, you will touch nothingness
be confused, have a pretext to find refuge
and, finally, watch the rain from the window.

El viento de los náufragos

****

Barefoot so as not to awaken you
you obey your pyramid prophecy
untouched soul
body without magic
foreign letters , that's what I am—you ask
and for the first time, you doubt

*   *   *   *

I pursue your smell
like I would for a word that hurts
like the cold and the rings under my eyes
flooding me
now all the air is your smell
asphyxiated from you I open
in my mouth
the paralytic letters
of your name

*   *   *   *

without permanence
without a son from your bed sheet
death calls and
will take you away untouched

*   *   *   *

Desde las fosas comunes
las desaparecidas, las borradas
las amadas del desamor
las que enterraste dentro tuyo
las de tu propio cementerio
empiezan una canción
tal vez un brazo alcance su mano
la reconozca suya
tal vez estén fundando un idioma
tal vez ordenen su cuerpo, su alma
tal vez
dicen. . .

3 nombres para un lugar

****

I

La gemelas nacen en un mundo par
aman por eso
el encuentro de las costillas
crecen en anverso y reverso
dejan siempre una silla vacía a su lado
no necesitan del agua para llamar a Narciso
ellas
las amantes de lo dual
inventan el cerco perfecto
danzan sobre el fuego de la balanza
hablan con su fantasma
se ríen de tu sombra
y de tu miedo al doblez

*   *   *   *

Hazme de nuevo
invéntame con otro barro
sin costillas ajenas
créame antes de luz y agua
para nunca depender de ellas
antes de mares y cielo
para habitar todo el azul
antes de separar noche y día
antes de heredarme gobiernos
sobre animales, árboles, cuarzos
hazme otra vez
menos tuya

From the mass graves
the disappeared, the ones wiped out
those beloved by indifference
the ones you buried within yourself
the ones of your own cemetery
begin a song
perhaps an arm can reach their hand
and recognize it as its own
perhaps they are founding a language
perhaps they are arranging their bodies, their souls
perhaps
they say. . .

3 nombres para un lugar

****

I

The twins are born in an equal world
that's why they love
the encounter of ribs
they grow on heads and tails
they always leave an empty chair by their side
they don't need water to fetch Narcissus
they
the lovers of duality
invent the perfect fence
they dance upon the fire of the scale
they speak with their ghost
they laugh at their shadow
and at your fear of duplicity.

*   *   *   *

Make me again
invent me with another clay
without an outsider's ribs
create me even before light and water
so as never to depend on them
before the seas and the skies
to inhabit everything blue
before separating night and day
before I inherit governance
over animals, trees, quartz
make me again
less yours

sin clavarme muerte o matanza
sin decirme que nada es cierto
hazme de papel
de palabras

*   *   *   *

Vendrá un día
y le hablaré de estas palabras
que contra ella escribo
Cuando debas conocer el miedo
el temor del cuerpo
quieto
el dolor de dejarme ir
pide a la vida por mi última caída
pide que sea suave
que el frío no me hunda
pide que sea otro desliz
que vuelva a la luz con otro cuerpo
y pueda reconocerte

Fronteras de doble filo

****

CONJUROS CONTRA LA TRISTEZA

Puedo ahora vender tu cuerpo al peor postor
vigilar personalmente que se empapen tus sábanas
    y que gires y grites y gimas toda la noche
entre piernas inclementes abrirte ante mil extraños
    encargarme de que te guste hasta que lo implores
    pasarte por la piel los que demoran el latido,
        los que llegan pronto
        los que tienen miedo
        los que se van
puedo llenarte de lentejuelas y escotes de esquina
    darte un disfraz, una lengua insaciable,
        unas manos que aprieten
    una paciencia terca de los dedos en tus nervios
un líquido inundando cada tanto tu veinte hambriento
        puedo mandar quien te sacie
entonces, tal vez, se te iría el horror a lo vulnerable.

*   *   *   *

without pinning me with death or killing
without telling me nothing is certain
make me of paper
of words

*   *   *   *

It will come some day
and I'll speak to it about these words
that it's against it that I write
When you have to meet fear
The dread of the body,
silent,
the pain of letting myself go
plead with life for my last fall
ask that it be soft
that the cold not overwhelm me
ask that I be another error
that I return to the light with another body
and that I recognize you.

Fronteras de doble filo

****

INCANTATIONS AGAINST SADNESS

I am now able to sell your body to the lowest bidder
   to personally check that your bed sheets get wet
      that you spin and cry and moan all night long
         between inclement legs, opening yourself
            to a thousand strangers
         to see that you like it, that you beg for it
      to pass your flesh to those with a slow pulse
            those who come quickly
               those who are afraid
               those who take off
I can regale you with sequins and low necklines
      give you a disguise, an insatiable tongue,
            some hands that squeeze
   a stubborn patience of fingers on your nerves
   a liquid drowning every so often your hungry belly
   I can order someone to satisfy you, then, perhaps,
your horror of all that's vulnerable would leave you.

*   *   *   *

DESAPARECIDO SUR (V)

Dos que no se hablaron nunca se abrazan.
Dos diferentes como sus siglos se miran,
adivinan en sus caras que la muerte ronda.
Uno se persigna, el otro corre por calles desiertas
antes de la hora marcada.

*   *   *   *

DESAPARECIDO SUR (VI)

Ella vivía de las costuras.
La tela se unía con alfileres.
La aguja seguía la línea marcada.
Ahora ella es la tela que alguien interroga.
Su sangre es la huella recién lavada.

*   *   *   *

HECHICERA (I)

Apenas abrí los ojos, ahí estaban ellos, los muertos
ignorantes todavía de su propio morir,
o los otros, los vientos amantes de la muerte
en cuyo mirar la vida era siempre más aguda;
unos adelantan la despedida de sus cuerpos
y andan sus palabras buscando mensajeros del después,
otros ya agotados equivocan las sendas del no retorno
y se refugian refunfuñando en muecas que da miedo ver
suelen venir a recostarse a mi sombra
con olor a pena reciente y madera encerada.
Mi mano, que ya les conoce el modo,
toma con prisa el dictado de lo pendiente.
Hay heridas hondas—me dicen—necesitadas de decirse.
Es el frío el que inaugura mis ojos,
el frío de los muertos que me visitan.

*   *   *   *

HECHICERA (III)

Y un día tenía la muerte en los pulmones,
apresando el tránsito del respiro
mi madre tiende puentes al sol
y caza para mí un poco de aire

DISAPPEARED SOUTH (V)

Two, who never spoke to one another, embrace.
Two, as different as their centuries, look at each other,
they recognize in their expressions that death approaches.
One makes the sign of the cross; the other runs through
deserted streets before the time comes.

*   *   *   *

DISAPPEARED SOUTH (VI)

She made a living by her sewing.
The fabric was joined with pins.
The needle followed the marked line.
Now she is the fabric that someone interrogates.
Her blood is the mark, newly cleaned.

*   *   *   *

SORCERESS (I)

I hardly opened my eyes, there they were,
the dead ones, still unaware of their demise,
or the others, the winds so loving of death,
in whose gaze life was always sharper;
some move up the farewell of their bodies and their
words wander, searching for messengers from beyond,
others, so fatigued, err on the paths of no return,
taking refuge and grumbling with faces a fright to see
they usually come to lean back on my shadow
with the smell of recent sorrow and waxed wood.
My hand, so familiar with their ways,
quickly takes dictation of pending matters.
There are deep wounds—they say—needful of telling.
It's the cold that inaugurates my eyes,
the cold of the dead who visit me.

*   *   *   *

SORCERESS (III)

And one day death in her lungs,
seizing the passage of breathing
my mother lays out bridges to the sun
and hunts for a bit of air for me

182

pero todo es vano
una vez habitado el umbral,
no se vive más sin estar un poco muerta.

El viento de los náufragos

****

HIJA DE MEDEA, 13

Cómplice de mi madre cuando es la otra
vi fascinada un velo corroer un cuerpo y un engaño
Colgué la cuerda y di ánimo a mis hermanos.
Tensé el nudo con la misma ceguera del demasiado amor.
Vengado en el padre el abandono de todo amante.
Con la misma urgencia de hombre amado
latiendo en la vértebra
con el mismo afán de que alguien nos salvara, así salvé
sacudí todo camino de los pies
todo buen final del desamor.

*   *   *   *

HIJA DE MEDEA, 31

Yo, tu hija muerta,
vuelvo de la muerte para amar la impotencia
para enseñarte a dejar ir, para aprender a perder. . .
para perdonarte,
coser las que fuiste
y juntas devolver la sombra
al Sol.

*   *   *   *

HIJA DE MEDEA, 40

Abre la oscuridad, mamá.
Ciérrame los ojos.

Hija de Medea

****

but it's all futile
once the threshold is occupied, one doesn't live
much longer without being a little dead.

El viento de los náufragos

****

MEDEA'S DAUGHTER, 13

Accomplice of my mother when it's the other one
fascinated, I saw a veil corrode a body and a deceit
I hung up the cord and encouraged my brothers.
I tightened the noose with the same blindness of too much love.
The abandonment of every lover avenged on the father.
With the same urgency of a beloved man
beating in my vertebrae
with the same fervor of someone saving us, so I saved,
I shook off all the road dust from my feet,
all of it, a good ending for indifference.

*   *   *   *

MEDEA'S DAUGHTER, 31

I, your dead daughter,
return from death to love helplessness
to teach you to let go, to learn to lose. . .
to pardon you,
to sew together the ones you were
and together to return the shadow
to the Sun.

*   *   *   *

MEDEA'S DAUGHTER, 40

Open the darkness, mother.
Close my eyes.

Hija de Medea

****

14

Blanca Wiethüchter

CRECERÁN LOS FUEGOS

En imágenes ocultas
un sol derramado esconde secretos
más hondos que el frío
agazapado en su sombra.

Extraño diálogo junto al vino
recuperando los rostros conocidos
avidez despierta en cada gesto
la alianza de los días de fiesta.

Distante
un amigo,
una ciudad,
un tiempo aguardan

Un torrente de ascuas permanece.
En las esquinas crecerán los fuegos,
polvo y arcilla.
Queda un abrazo
recogido en la altura.

Asistir al tiempo

****

Orgullo de ser
        blanco
para una bala

*   *   *   *

¿Será ésta la herida que nos nombra pueblo?

Noviembre 79

****

SIN CRÓNICAS

Nosotros que somos responsables de vivir
y hemos nacido en el tercer mundo.
Nosotros que pedimos justicia
y vivimos en América del Sur.
Nosotros que morimos en Bolivia

THE FIRES WILL GROW

In hidden images
a scattered sun hides secrets
deeper than the cold
crouched in its shadow.

A peculiar dialog with wine
recovering familiar faces
avidness awakens in every gesture
the alliance of holidays.

Far away,
a friend,
a city,
a time all await.

A torrent of embers remains.
On street corners, fires, ash, and clay
will grow.
There remains an embrace
gathered on the summit.

Asistir al tiempo

****

The pride of being
        the target
for a bullet

*   *   *   *

This wound: can this be what calls us a nation?

Noviembre 79

****

WITHOUT CHRONICLES

We who are responsible for living
and have been born in the third world.
We who ask for justice
and live in South America.
We who die in Bolivia

únicos y desolados.
Somos esa historia que no se escribe
y que camina con la cabeza cortada.

*   *   *   *

Muere un estudiante con un tiro en la espalda.
La sangre derramada
se esparce en la calle
como un grito.
¿Quién puede escribir sobre la inocencia?

Travesía

****

EL FULGOR -- 3

Palmo a palmo
tiento las paredes del día.
Obstinada
toco las murallas de la noche.
En alguna parte, en algún lugar
presiento el hueco negro
por el que con un salto
me deslizaré al otro lado.
Al antiguo valle
          a la tierra libre
horizonte poblado
          de montañas como templos
          de hombres andando
                    en las noches sagradas.
Ese hueco invisible
ese ojo negro que alumbra
el nombre de la vida
con el soplo de otro viento.

Aguzas el oído
          la voz que te piensa y acompaña:
¡Quiero la vida
          y que la muerte
                    no me muera!

El rigor de la llama

****

unique and desolate.
We are that history that doesn't get written
and that walks about with its head cut off.

*   *   *   *

A student dies, shot in the back.
Spilled blood
spreads in the street
like a cry.
Who can write about innocence?

Travesía

****

SPLENDOR -- 3

Little by little
I touch the walls of day.
Obstinate,
I touch the city walls of night.
Somewhere, some place
I foresee the black hollow
through which with one leap
I'll slip over to the other side.
To the ancient valley
        to the free land
a horizon filled with
            mountains like temples
            men walking about
                on sacred nights.
That invisible hollow
that black eye that illuminates
the name of life
with the breath of another wind.

You sharpen your ears
    the voice that accompanies and thinks of you:
I want life,
        but I don't want death
            to die on me!

El rigor de la llama

****

*   *   *   *

Tras la amarilla espesura de retamas
un jardinero
no ajeno al goce de la niña descalza
agasaja su rosa
danzante mariposa
en manos de un jardinero
centinela del placer.
Alada
       descubre alta
la corona de un vuelo real.

     Tras la oscura espesura
     de grandes palabras que asustan
     un verbo
     no ajeno al miedo
     de la niña descalza
     amordaza su lengua.
     Y el silencio, cómplice
     celebra sordo al espanto
     la corona de un mudo funeral.

La lagarta

****

TERCER DÍA

Casi ya de madrugada
deshice cama y también veladores
guardé edredones, sábanas y joyas,
como siempre en aquella alacena.
Cambié el delicado camisón de lino damasquino
por uno más sereno hilado en casta lana blanca.
Por la tarde me dormí llena de conjeturas siniestras
y otra vez en el sueño
—esa oscura ley que me castiga—
vi a Ulises amando a Circe la hechicera
—por cierto, qué mujer más bella.
Al despertar, mudé los muebles de lugar
para empezar un no sé qué con otro orden.
Y, ahí estaba, hila que te hila
escribe que te escribe
teje que te teje.
En mi balcón de costura
deshilo desescribo, destejo

*   *   *   *

Behind the yellow thickness of broom shrubs
a gardener
not beyond enjoying a barefoot girl
regales his rose,
a dancing butterfly
that in the hands of a gardener
is a sentinel of pleasure.
Winged,
     it discovers up high
the crown of a royal flight.

     Behind the dark thicket
     of big words that frighten,
     a verb,
     not foreign to the fear
     of the barefoot girl,
     clamps down her tongue.
     And the silence, an accomplice,
     celebrates, deaf to the terror,
     the wreath of a mute funeral.

     La lagarta

****

THIRD DAY

Almost at the break of dawn
I undid the bed, and with the candlesticks
I put away eiderdowns, sheets, and jewels,
as usual, in that closet.
I exchanged the delicate damascened nightshirt
for a quieter one, stitched in a chaste, white wool.
In the afternoon I slept full of evil conjectures
and again in a dream
—that dark law that punishes me—
I saw Ulysses loving Circe the sorceress
—for sure, what a beautiful woman.
On awakening, I moved around the furniture
to begin, who knows what, another arrangement.
And there it was, spinning and spinning,
writing and writing,
weaving and weaving.
On my balcony for sewing,
I unravel, I un-write, I unweave

sin comprender qué naufragio interior
el que no me permite hilar
a Ulises,
                    en la isla,
                                        aquí,
                                                        conmigo.
Pero de súbito, Penélope mi hermana,
despierto en otro sueño
veo
            otra
                    la trama:
                    una hebra que se tuerce
                    un hilo que se muerde
                    un verbo que hace falta
y comprendo, por qué no llega nunca aquel que espero.
¡El conjuro, el conjuro convoca el gesto inverso!
El hilo se desata
el sueño se desueña
la canción se desencanta
parezco una valija desvalijada
una nada.
Soy un cuento que ya no cuenta
el regreso de Ulises a Itaca.
¿Qué hacer, dime, si Ulises vuelve ahora?

                              Ítaca

****

El silencio
                    es un pájaro
en el aire
                    una espada.

*   *   *   *

La naturaleza despierta en mí
al contemplarla
esa nostalgia antigua
de ser con los seres
aquel instante
                    sin otro instante
el único
            el solo
                    cielo posible.
*   *   *   *

without understanding what interior shipwreck
is the one that doesn't let me spin
Ulysses,
       on the island,
              here,
                   with me.
But suddenly, Penelope, my sister,
I awake in another dream
I see
       another one
            the plot:
a fiber that gets twisted
a thread that gets snagged
a verb that's missing
and I understand why the one I'm waiting for
never arrives. The incantation. The incantation
summons the opposite action.
The thread unravels
the dream un-dreams itself
the song un-sings itself
I seem like a valise emptied by robbery, a nothing.
I am a story that no longer tells
the return of Ulysses to Ithaca.
What would I do, tell me, if Ulysses returns now?

                       Ítaca

****

Silence
       is a bird
in the air
       a sword.

*   *   *   *

Nature awakens in me
when I contemplate it
that old nostalgia
of being with beings
that instant
       no other instant
the one
       the only
           possible sky.
*   *   *   *

Aquí
donde crecen los mangos y los papayos
donde año tras año se desborda el río
y el verde no es un color
sino la voluntad ruidosa
de ocultos ecos y cansancios.

Aquí
en la densa espesura de la selva
la profundidad es un grito
de algo
que está por nacer.

El verde no es un color

****

RAPSODIA SEXTA

En otro cuarto, escaleras arriba
oigo el respirar profundo
del más grande de los silencios
sorda al estruendo que hacen al caer
los custodios del tiempo de mi madre
que es muerta.
Me deslizo: presente puro mi madre
colocada a la luz del día,
poderosamente muerta.
Ni más acá ni más allá, aquí, en este lugar
desembarca mi madre
apasionadamente muerta.
Lágrimas acampan en estos suelos
y ahora sé que no existe más orilla
que este océano de luz
traspasando el país a raudales.

Ya nada parece un sueño.
Alaba el mundo y nunca sueñes, me digo
que el soñar trae presunciones
soberbia y demonios en reyerta.

Angeles del miedo

****

Here
where the mangos and papayas grow
where year after year the river overflows
and where green is not a color
but rather a noisy will
of hidden echoes and fatigue.

Here
in the dense thicket of the forest
profoundness is a cry
        from something
                        about to be born.

El verde no es un color

****

SIXTH RHAPSODY

In another room upstairs
I hear the deep breathing
of the greatest of all silences
deaf to the clamor made by the fall of the custodians
who keep the time left for my mother,
who is dead.
I slip: in the pure present, my mother
placed in broad daylight,
powerfully dead.
Not more here nor there, here, in this place
my mother disembarks
passionately dead.
Tears camp down on these grounds
and now I know no other shore exists
beside this ocean of light
passing through the country in torrents.

Now nothing seems like a dream.
Praise the world and never dream, I tell myself
that dreaming brings presumption,
arrogance, and quarreling demons.

Ángeles del miedo

****

Si tú te mueres primero amor
ay, si tú te mueres primero
si eso ocurriera ya no habría árbol que tocara el cielo
ni puerta que mirara al campo
y la calle se truncaría con el sólo andar de mis pies.

*   *   *   *

Si yo muero primero amor es necesario dejar dicho,
que fue el prodigio de tu presencia iluminada
tu abrazo, tu mano, tu pie de tranco largo
el germen, el enigma, de todas mis palabras
el más grande sortilegio que diera la aurora.

*   *   *   *

Entonces, si por la gracia de la vida eres verbo,
oh dulce amor,
si yo muero primero, ay, si yo muero primero
me hallarás encaramada sobre el más alto faro
atenta a las olas
              regresar nuestra hoguera.

Luminar

(Blanca Wiethüchter, 1947-2004)

****

If you die first, my love, ah, if you die first
if that happened, no longer would there be a tree
that could touch the sky
nor a door that could open to a field
and the street would truncate with just
the steps of my feet.

*   *   *   *

If I die first, love, it's necessary to leave a message
that it was the prodigy of your glowing presence,
your embrace, your hand, the foot of your long stride
the germ, the enigma, of all of my words
the greatest magic spell that the aurora could offer.

*   *   *   *

Then, if for the grace of life you are the word,
oh sweet love,
if I die first, ah, if I die first
you will find me perched atop the tallest lighthouse
attentive to the waves
                    to return our bonfire.

Luminar

(Blanca Wiethüchter, 1947-2004)

****

THE POETS AND THEIR BIBLIOGRAPHIES

JORGE CAMPERO

The early poetry of Jorge Campero (Tarija, Bolivia, 1953) was scarcely published: beginning with the 1970s cultural review *Desnudando Tu Ciudad*, of the literary group Luz Ácida, and afterwards in *Espacio Cultural AveSol*. In some cases, only a dozen copies of his works were in circulation, and today they are virtually non-existent. Since then, he began publishing his collected poems and his renown has grown to the point where he has been accorded Bolivia's most prestigious award for poetry in successive years: the Premio Nacional de Poesía Yolanda Bedregal in 2001 for *Musa en jeans descolorido*, and again in 2002 for *Jaguar azul*.

Campero has earned a living in a variety of trades, lived in Bolivia's Chaco region for a while, but has dedicated his meaningful time to literary endeavors such as directing the literary review *Camarada Máuser* (1982), co-directing of the newspaper, *El Telégrafo* and of the poetry review *Siesta Nacional* (1988), and co-editing the literary review *El Cielo de las serpientes* (1994). He currently resides in La Paz.

POETRY

Promiscuas. La Paz: Author's ed., 1976.
A boca de jarro. La Paz: Author's ed., 1979.
Árbol eventual. La Paz: Paternos, 1983.
Svmarivm comvn sobre vivos. La Paz: Tándem, 1985.
El cielo de las serpientes. La Paz: Los Jinetes del Apocalipsis, 1994.
El corazón ardiente. La Paz: Author's ed. 2001.
Musa en jeans descolorido. La Paz: Ministerio de Educación, Cultura y Deportes / Plural, 2001.
Jaguar azul. La Paz: Ministerio de Educación, Cultura y Deportes / Plural, 2002.

Poeta sin Pedigree. La Paz: Author's ed. (2002).
Árbol eventual. Poemas 1979-1984. La Paz: Plural, 2009.

CRITICISM, REVIEWS AND INTERVIEWS

Arzoumanian, Ana. "*Jaguar Azul* de Jorge Campero." Review. *Fondo Negro* (*La Prensa*, La Paz) 12 June 2005: 5.

Badani, Javier. "La desilusión es la musa del poeta tarijeño Jorge Campero." *Tendencias* (*La Razón*, La Paz) 10 July 2005: C1.

Bajo, Ricardo. "Tregua para un maldito." *Fondo Negro* (*La Prensa*, La Paz) 25 Nov. 2001: 1-2.

Barriga, Julio. "Jorge Campero ¿poeta tarijeno?" *Cultura* (*Nuevo Sur*, Tarija, Bolivia) 9 Dec. 2001: 4A.

Basualdo, Marco. "Campero, Premio Nacional de Poesía: Defendí bien mi título." *Cultura* (*La Prensa*, La Paz) 27 Nov. 2002: 9b.

Behoteguy, Solange. "En busca de la 'tierra sin mal.' El regreso del jaguar azul." Rev. of *Jaguar Azul*, by Jorge Campero. *Brújula* (Santa Cruz) 30 Nov. 2002: 4.

—. "El premio nacional de Poesía Yolanda Bedregal le tocó a un guerrero que busca la 'tierra sin mal.'" *Fondo Negro* (*La Prensa*, La Paz) 1 Dec. 2002: 1-2.

Campero, Jorge. "Jorge Campero: 'He apostado al caballo cojo.'" Interview with Germán Araúz Crespo. *Cultura y Ocio* (*Pulso*, La Paz) 20-26 Dec. 2002: 20.

—. "Jorge Campero y la poesía: Esa amante caprichosa." Interview with Ricardo Herrera." *Brújula* (*El Deber*, Santa Cruz) 26 Dec. 2002: 1-3.

Granados, Pedro. "Ensayo sobre poesía boliviana." http://www. ecdotica.com/2008/05/09/ensayo-sobre-la- poesia-boliviana/

Herrera, Ricardo. "Jorge Campero: 'La poesía es una mujer celosa.'" *Brújula* (*El Deber*, Santa Cruz) 21 Dec. 2002: 1-3.

"*Jaguar azul* entre los 10 mejores libros de América Latina en XII Feria del Libro de La Habana." *La Ciudad* (*La Prensa*, La Paz) 7 Feb. 2004: b8.

"Jorge Campero gana otra vez el Premio Nacional de Poesía." *Cultura* (*La Prensa*, La Paz) 26 Nov. 2002: 9b.

"Jorge Campero, ganador reincidente del Bedregal." *Cultura* (*La Razón*, La Paz) 27 Nov. 2002: A 23.

"Jorge Campero y Juan Carlos Orihuela viajaron al norte de Chile." http://www.letras.s5.com/jc201005.htm

Mercado, Edmundo. "Un poeta dueño del destino de su canto."

Musa en jeans descolorido, by Jorge Campero. La Paz: Ministerio de Educación, Cultura y Deportes / Plural: 2001. Inside dust cover.

—. "Un poeta dueño del destino de su canto." *Jaguar azul*, by Jorge
Campero. La Paz: Ministerio de Educación, Cultura y Deportes / Plural: 2002. Inside dust covers.

"La musa de Jorge Campero desciende sobre la ciudad." *La Razón* (La Paz) 9 Sep. 2001: A26.

Navia, Mónica. "Poesía desde el minibús: La contemplación como ser." Instituto Normal Superior Simón Bolívar-La Paz: 1-4.

"La poesía en los concursos es mala o regular." http://www.bolivia. com /noticias/autonoticias/DetalleNoticia18665.asp

Quirós, J. "Arbol eventual." Review. *Signo* 15 (1985): 174.

Vera Jordán, Antonio. "Jorge Campero: Animal de las veredas." *El Juguete Rabioso* (La Paz) 3 Mar. 2002: 3.

Zelaya Sánchez, Martín. "Campero paseó a su jaguar en Argentina." Rev. of *Jaguar Azul*, by Jorge Campero. *Fondo Negro* (*La Prensa*, La Paz) 12 June 2005: 1; 4-5.

"28/03: Chairo con alguna notable poesía boliviana última." http:// blog.pucp.edu.pe/item/20981

****

BENJAMÍN CHÁVEZ

Benjamín Chávez (Santa Cruz, Bolivia, 1971) spent his youth in Oruro, where he published his first two books of poetry. He received the Luis Mendizábal Santa Cruz Prize for his first book, *Prehistorias del androide* (1994), and was a finalist for the "Premio Nacional de Poesía Yolanda Bedregal" in 2003 for his book *Y allá en lo alto un pedazo de cielo*. For his book, *Pequeña libería de viejo* (2006), he was awarded the National Award for Poetry "Yolanda Bedregal." His poems have appeared in numerous national print media and in anthologies. He collaborates in the literary review, "La Mariposa Mundial," and is a member of the editorial staff of the literary supplement "El Duende" in Oruro, Bolivia. He coedited an anthology of young Bolivian poets: *Cambio climático: panorama de la joven Poesía boliviana* (2009). Chávez was a special guest of the Festival Internacional de Poesía in Medellín in July 2008. He currently resides in La Paz.

POETRY

Prehistorias del androide. Oruro, Bolivia: Fundacion Cultural
    FEPO, 1994.
Con la misma tijera. Oruro: Author's ed., 1999.
Santo sin devoción. La Paz: Plural, 2000.
Y allá en lo alto un pedazo de cielo. La Paz: Plural, 2003.
Extramuros. La Paz: La Mariposa Mundial / Plural, 2004.
Pequeña Librería de viejo. La Paz: Plural, 2007.
Manual de contemplación (Anthology). La Paz: Author's ed., 2008.

CRITICISM, REVIEWS, INTERVIEWS

Cáceres, Beto. "Ganador del Premio Nacional de Poesía Yolanda
    Bedregal, 2006." 14 Dec. 2006. http://estanteboliviano.
    blogspot.com/2006/12/ganador-del-premio—nacional-de-
    poesa.html
Chávez, Benjamín. "El lenguaje poético es el más certero."
    Interview with Michel Zelada Cabrera. *Lecturas* (*Los
    Tiempos.com*, La Paz, 1 Apr. 2007): http://www. lostiempos.
    com/lecturas/01-04-07/arte.php
—. "Entrevista con Benjamín Chávez. De tu baúl de misterios."
    XVIII Festival Internacional de Poesía de Medellín (Colombia)
    2008: Interview. http://www.festival depoesiademedellin.org/
    pub.php/es/Festival/XVIII_Festival/chavez.html
—. "Entrevista al poeta boliviano Benjamín Chávez . . ." Interview with
    Javier Claure Covarrubias. Quaderns digital.net (2003): http://
    www.quadernsdigitals.net/index.php?accionMenu=secciones.
    VisualizaArticuloSeccionIU.visualiza&proyecto_
    id=2&articuloSeccion_id=7549
Echavarren, Roberto. "Acerca de *Pequeña librería de viejo*." Review.
    Pequeña librería de viejo, by Benjamín Chávez. La Paz:
    Plural, 2007. 91.
Ortiz, Rodolfo. "Benjamín Chávez, Premio Nacional de Poesía."
    Revista La Mariposa Mundial (La Paz) 16-17 (2007).
—. [No title.] *Extramuros*, by Benjamín Chávez. La Paz: Plural,
    2004. Back cover.

Quiroga, Juan Carlos Ramiro. [No title] *Revista Mar con Soroche* (La Paz, Bolivia; Santiago, Chile) 1 (2006).

—. [No title.] *Y allá en lo alto un pedazo de cielo*, by Benjamín Chávez. La Paz: Plural, 2003. Back cover.

—. "Vidas domésticas: Benjamín Chávez y Sergio Parra." Proyecto Patrimonio (Santiago, Chile): http://letras.s5.com.istemp.com /sergioparra02803.htm

Tapia Anaya, Vilma. "Pequeña librería de viejo." *Revista La Mariposa Mundial* (La Paz) 16-17 (2007).

Vargas, Rubén. "Benjamín Chávez: Y allá en lo alto un pedazo de cielo." *Revista La Mariposa Mundial* (La Paz) 10 (2003): 61.

—. [No title.] *Santo sin devoción*, by Benjamín Chávez. La Paz: Plural, 2000. Back cover.

Velásquez Guzmán, Mónica. "Donde el mundo no me alcance. Acerca de *Pequeña Librería de viejo* de Benjamín Chávez." *Alejandría* (La Paz) 10 (2007): 15.

****

EDUARDO MITRE

Poet, essayist, and professor, Eduardo Mitre (Oruro, 1943) studied French literature in France, and received his Ph.D. in Hispanic literatures at the University of Pittsburgh. Currently a professor of Latin American literature at St. John's University, Mitre is a member of the Academia Boliviana de la Lengua since 2000, and has written books of essays/anthologies devoted to recent Bolivian poetry: *El árbol y la piedra: Poetas contemporáneos de Bolivia* (1986); *El Aliento en las hojas: Otras voces de la poesía boliviana* (1998); *De cuatro constelaciones: Ensayo y antología* (1994); *Pasos y voces. Nueve poetas contemporáneos de Bolivia: Ensayos y Antología* (2010); and a literary study on Chilean poet Vicente Huidobro, *Huidobro, hambre de espacio y sed de ciel* (1981). Mitre has also compiled a bilingual anthology of Belgian poets, *Urnas y nupcias* (1998), and has been a contributor to the magazine *Vuelta*, and to *Letras libres*.

POETRY

Elegía a una muchacha. Cochabamba, Bolivia: Universidad Mayor de San Simón, 1965.

Morada. Caracas, Venezuela: Monte Avila, 1975.

Ferviente humo. Cochabamba, Bolivia: Ediciones Portales, 1976. 3rd. ed. La Paz: Nuevo Milenio, 1998.

Mirabilia. La Paz: Colegio Don Bosco, 1979. 2$^{nd.}$ ed. (revised and augmented.) Illustrations Romanet Zárate Márquez. Santa Cruz de la Sierra, Bolivia: El País, 2010.

Razón ardiente. La Paz: Altiplano,1983.

Desde tu cuerpo. La Paz: Altiplano, 1984.

El peregrino y la ausencia. La Paz: Altiplano, 1988.

La luz del regreso. Cochabamba: Fundación Simón I. Patiño, 1990.

Líneas de otoño. Mexico City: Los Caprichos/Imagen Arte, 1993.

Carta a la inolvidable. Cochabamba: Funcación Simón I. Patiño, 1996.

Camino de cualquier parte. Madrid: Visor, 1998.

Antología poética (Audio CD). Cochabamba: Fundación Simón I. Patiño, 2000.

El paraguas de Manhattan. Valencia: Pre-Textos, 2004.

Versi d'autunno. Venice, Italy: Sinopia, 2005.

Vitrales de la memoria. Valencia, Spain: Pre-Textos, 2007.

Al paso del instante. Valencia, Spain: Pre-Textos, 2009.

Celebraciones. Illus. Luis Mayo. Madrid, Spain: Estampa, 2011.

CRITICISM, REVIEWS, INTERVIEWS

Antezana Juárez, Luis. "Palabras, espacios y cuerpos." *Elementos de semiótica literaria.* La Paz: Instituto Boliviano de Cultura, 1977. 94-107.

—. *Ensayos y lecturas.* La Paz: Altiplano, 1986. 265-295.

—. "Luis Antezana habla de Mitre." *Los Tiempos* (Cochabamba) 23 Feb. 1994.

Encuentro: Diálogos sobre escritura y mujeres. La Paz: Sierpe, 1999.

Falconi, José Luis and José Antonio Mazzotti. *The other Latinos: Central and South Americans in the United States.* Cambridge, Ma.; London: Harvard UP, 2010.

Martins, Floriano. *Escritura conquistada: diálogos com escritores latino-americanos.* Fortaleza, Brazil: Letra & Música Comunicação, 1998.

Mitre, Eduardo. "Entrevista con Eduardo Mitre." Interview by Alberto Julián Pérez. *Alba de América: Revista Literaria* 11:20-21 (1993): 489-495.

—. "Una conversación entre Eduardo Mitre y Marie-Lise Gazarian." Interview with Marie-Lise Gazarian. *Entre Rascacielos.* (St. John's University, Queens, N.Y.)15 (2008): 89-95.

Muñoz Molina, Antonio. "Eduardo Mitre: Assenze et ritorni." Trans. Claudio Cinti. *Poesia.* (Milan, Italy) 221 (2007): 49-51.

Paz Soldán, Edmundo. Rev. of *De cuatro constelaciones: Estudio y antología,* by Eduardo Mitre. *Revista de Crítica Literaria Latinoamericana* 23: 46 (1997): 370-372.

Pérez, Alberto Julián. "Eduardo Mitre." *Revolución poética y modernidad periférica: ensayos de poesía hispanoamericana.* Buenos Aires: Corregidor, 2009. 239-264.

Quinteros Soria, Juan. "La palabra 'dicha': Sobre la poesía de Eduardo Mitre." *Revista Iberoamericana* 52.134 (1986): 207-218.

Sucre, Guillermo. Prólogo. *Mirabilia.* 2nd. ed. Santa Cruz de la Sierra: El País, 2010.

Vargas, Claret. "The Persistence of Distance in the Poetry of Eduardo Mitre." *The Other Latinos.* Ed. José Luis Falconi and José Antonio Mazzotti. Cambridge, MA.; London, Great Britain: Harvard University David Rockefeller Center for Latin American Studies, 2007. 141-173.

****

JAIME NISTTAHUZ

Born in Carabuco, Provincia Camacho de La Paz, Bolivia in 1933 Jaime Nisttahuz is a poet, narrator, news reporter, film critic, and retired administrator in the Bolivian Social Security office of the Caja Ferriovaria. He has declared himself a lifelong hermit and "anarchosocialist" of La Paz who becomes invisible when he dons a hat. He co-edited the literary review *Trasluz*, published a novel, *Barriomundo* (1993), collections of short stories, *Fábulas contra la oscuridad* (1994) and *Cuentos desnudos* (2008) and has been a frequent contributor of short stories, reviews, "aforismos y desaforismos," and essays in local print media. His works have appeared in national and international anthologies, but he points out that many of his ideas have been pillaged, as if he were just giving them away. For example he's been developing a method for crystallizing creativity, and another for converting water into beer, so as not to be accused of copying Jesus Christ.

POETRY

Escrito en los muros. La Paz: Don Bosco, 1976.
El murmullo de las ropas. La Paz: Palabra Encendida, 1980.
Palabras con agujeros. La Paz: Palabra Encendida, 1983.
La humedad es una sombra y otros poemas. La Paz: UMSA, Carrera
    de Artes, 1992.
Recodo en el aire. La Paz: Plural, 2003.
Inquilinos del insomnio. La Paz: Gente Común, 2008.

A selection of poems in Spanish by Jaime Nisttahuz can be found at:
    http:www.boliviaweb.com/poetry/nisttahuz.htm

CRITICISM, REVIEWS AND INTERVIEWS

"*Escrito en los muros* de Jaime Nisttahuz." Review of *Escrito en los
    muros*. *El Diario* (La Paz) 21 Jan. 1979.
Gamarra Durana, Alfonso. "Nisttahuz camina sobre sí mismo."
    Presencia Literaria (La Paz) 1 Oct. 1989.
"Jaime Nisttahuz, escritor," *Presencia Literaria* (La Paz) 17 Aug.
    1994.
"Jaime Nisttahuz y la poesía: Lo que camina dentro." Interview.
    Cultura Hoy (La Paz) 10 Feb. 1995.
"Nisttahuz: 'Escribir es una enfermedad," Interview with Ricardo
    Bajo. *La Prensa* (La Paz) 20 Apr. 2003.

"La sociedad de los poetas vivos," Interview with C.A.R.R. *La Razón* (La Paz) 22 Dec. 1991: 10.

****

EDUARDO NOGALES GUZMÁN

Born in Oruro, Bolivia in 1959, Eduardo Nogales is a poet, essayist, social researcher and journalist. He won the National Literary Award for Poetry "Franz Tamayo" in 1998; the same award for short stories in 2003; the first prize in "Juegos Florales Nacionales" in Oruro in 1978; first prize in "Semanario Aquí" for poetry in La Paz, 1984; first prize in poetry in the "Premio Nacional en Poesía, Universidad Técnica de Oruro" in 1985, and honorary mentions in three other national awards for poetry. His poems are included in numerous national and international anthologies, and he has written two books of short stories: *El avión y la miel más otros cuentos* (2002) and *La balada del Peines y otros cuentos* (2004). Born in Oruro, Bolivia in 1957, he has since divided his time between Cochabamba and La Paz. He studied social communication at the Universidad Católica Boliviana; later worked as a journalist in television, radio, the press; and also in research in rural development, education and production in the Bolivian Andes and valleys.

POETRY

Raíces de ceniza viva. La Paz: Casa de la Cultura, 1978.
[With Eddy Quintana Lanza and Nicómedes Suárez.] *Poemas.* La
    Paz: Casa Municipal de la Cultura "Franz Tamayo," 1978.
La nave iluminada. La Paz: ERBOL / Educación Radiofónica de
    Bolivia, 1990.
La inquietud de los reinos. Oruro, Bolivia: Ediciones del Pez, 1995.
Los deseantes del arca. La Paz: Casa de la Cultura, 1998.
El jardín de las lentitudes. La Paz: Plural, 2003.
El último cabaret. La Paz: Plural, 2004.
El humo del paraíso: 2000-2003. La Paz: Plural / Fundación Yolanda
    Bedregal / Viceministerio de Cultura: 2005.

CRITICISM, REVIEWS, INTERVIEWS

"Aprueban el . . ." *La Prensa* (La Paz, 28 Oct. 2004): 11b.
Quiroga, J. C. [No title.] *La nave iluminada*, by Eduardo Nogales
    Guzmán. La Paz: Educación Radiofónica de Bolivia, 1990.
    Inside dust covers.
—. "La nave de los locos." *Presencia Literaria* 28.06 (1992): 3.

****

JUAN CARLOS ORIHUELA

Juan Carlos Orihuela (La Paz, 1952) is a poet, dramatist, musician, and professor emeritus at the Universidad Mayor de San Andres (La Paz, Bolivia), where he is currently the director of the literature program. As former director of the Instituto Nacional Universitario de Bolivia, he compiled ethnological studies on the role of women in Bolivian society. He received his Ph.D. in Hispanic-American literature at the University of California, Davis.

In 1991 he received the Award for Radio Drama from the Westdeutscher Rundfunk Koln (WDR) of Germany, and his work was subsequently broadcasted by radio in German, Flemish, and Spanish. He was awarded the Franz Tamayo National Poetry Prize in1981 for his book *De amor, piedras y destierro*. Orihuela has written numerous essays on Bolivian literature for books, magazines, and newspapers in Bolivia and abroad. His poems have been included in several anthologies, and since 2001, Orihuela has represented Bolivia in various international poetry events. Besides poetry, his other passion is composing songs; he has recorded five CDs, the latest being "Celebraciones" with Oscar García.

POETRY

De amor, piedras y destierro. La Paz: Altiplano, 1983.
Llalva / Los gemelos. La Paz: OFAVIM, 1995.
Febreros. La Paz: El Hombrecito Sentado, 1996. 2nd ed. La Paz:
    Hombrecito sentado, 2004.

Esa herencia. La Paz: Plural, 2000.
Cuerpos del cuerpo. La Paz: Plural, 2000.
Oficio del tiempo. La Paz: Plural, 2005.
Los cuatro elementos. La Paz: Funcación Simón I. Patiño, 2008.
Poemario de sensaciones. La Paz: Plural, 2009
Las horas del mundo. La Paz: Plural, 2010. [New and revised reprint of all of Orihuela's previous poetry in eight books.]

For a selection of Orihuela's poetry in Spanish, see:
http://festivalinternacionaldepoesiaenpuertorico.com/juancarlosorihu
ela.html
http://www.publications.villanova.edu/naufragios/2010-02/poesia/
juancarlos-orihuela-1012.html

CRITICISM, REVIEWS, INTERVIEWS

Antenanza, H. "Hilvanando la memoria . . ." *Presencia / Linterna* (27 Oct. 1991): 5.
"Orihuela lanza su antología poética personal." *La Razón* (La Paz) 19 Aug. 2010:http://www.la-azon.com/version.php?ArticleId =116197&EditionId=2258
Vargas, Rubén. "Sobre Oficio del tiempo, de Juan Carlos Orihuela." *Fondo Negro (La Prensa, La Paz)*, 24 Jul. 2005.
Velásquez, Mónica. "El cuerpo como espacio social." *Tendencias (La Razón, La Paz)* 11 Apr. 2004.
—. "Un paseo por la poesía boliviana desde mediados del siglo XX." *Nuestra América. Revista de Estudios sobre la Cultura Latinoamericana 3 Porto, Portugal: U Fernando Pessoa, 2007.*
—. "Un paseo por la poesía boliviana." *Alforja: Revista de poesía 43* U Autónoma de Sinaloa, México, 2007.
—. "El vaivén duplicado del deseo." Rev. of *Febreros,* by Juan Carlos Orihuela. *Presencia Literaria* (La Paz) 25 Aug. 1996.

****

HUMBERTO QUINO MÁRQUEZ

This poet practices levitation and open rebellion. He is a mystic without a god, unpatriotic, vegetarian, and a book addict. Humberto Quino Márquez (La Paz, 1950) studied philosophy at the Universidad Mayor de San Andrés (La Paz) and possibly graduated in 1989. He was director of various short-lived literary and cultural reviews over the years—*Humus literario; Papel Higiénico; Dador; El Sueño de la Razón; Tiro al Aire*; and *La Torre de los Locos*—and founder of *Camarada Máuser*. Quino previously lived in Peru and Spain. His poems have been included in literary magazines and anthologies throughout Latin America and Europe, and have been translated to several languages. In addition to his published works of poetry, he has published *Diccionario herético* (1993), a novel, *El diablo predicador* (1983), and two anthologies of other poets: *Álbum de la nueva poesía chilena* (1994); and *Fosa común: Antología* (1985) on Bolivian poets. He currently resides in La Paz.

POETRY

Escritura fallida. Lima: Arte / Reda, 1976.
Delirio de un fauno en la avenida Buenos Aires a las 12 & 45. Lima: Arte/Reda 1978.
Balada para mi coronel Claribel y otros huevos. La Paz: Author's ed., 1979.
Manual de esclavos. La Paz: Author's ed., 1980
Mudanza de oficio. La Paz: Author's ed., 1983.
Fosa común: La Paz: Ediciones del Taller, 1985.
Tratado sobre la superstición de los mortales. La Paz: La oveja descarriada, 1987.
Crítica de la pasión pura. La Paz: Papeles de Acracia, 1993.
Summa poética. La Paz: Plural, 2002
Coitus ergo sum. La Paz: CIMA, 2003.
Ópera parca. Antología personal. La Paz: Plural, 2011.

Also, for a selection of his poetry in Spanish, see:
http://www.festivaldepoesiademedellin.org/pub.php/ en/Revista/ ultimas_ediciones/62_63/quino.html

http://laseleccionesafectivasbolivia.blogspot.com/2007/08/humberto-quino-mrquez.html

http://www.litterae.cl/quinopoemas.html

http://laseleccionesafectivasbolivia.blogspot.com/2007/08/humberto-quino-mrquez.html

CRITICISM, REVIEWS, INTERVIEWS

Antezana J, Luis H. "Sobre una crítica a la pasión pura." *Signo: Cuadernos Bolivianos de Cultura* (La Paz) 41 (1994): 65-82.

Chávez, Benjamín. "Coitos ergo sum." Review. *Mariposa Mundial* 11/12 (2003-2004): 75.

Francovich, G. "Tres humoristas." *Zorro Antonio* 8 (1991): 11.

Mitre, Eduardo. *El aliento de las hojas.* La Paz: Plural, 1998.

Quino, Humberto. "La Poesía: La anarquía y la purficación." Interview with Leonardo García-Pavón and Blanca Wiethüchter. *Hipótesis* (La Paz) IV. 1 (1994): 3-14.

—. "La ópera parca de Humberto Quino." Interview with Sebastián Antezana. La Paz: La Prensa.com.bo, 8 July 2011: http://www.laprensa.com.bo/diario/entretendencias/cultura/20110807/la-opera-parca-de-humberto-quino_2876_5437.html

—. "La ópera parca de Humberto Quino." Interview. La Paz: #poesía, 8 Ago. 2011. http://www.poesia-irc.com/j/index.php?option=com_content&view=article&id=8673%3Ala-opera-parca-de-humberto-quino&catid=15%3Anoticias-general&Itemid=18

—. "La feria sufre una proverbial carestía de buena literatura." Interview. La Paz: Página Siete.bo, 5 Aug. 2011: http://www.paginasiete.bo/2011-08-06/Cultura/ NoticiaPrincipal/26Cul00206.aspx

Quiroga, Juan Carlos. "La palestra y la fosa: Humberto Quino." *Summa poética*, by Humberto Quino. La Paz: Plural, 2002. 133-137.

—. "Un álbum de la poesía chilena en Bolivia." Proyecto Patrimonio, 2004: http://www.letras.s5.com/Quiroga 300104.htm

****

MARÍA SOLEDAD QUIROGA

Poet and narrator, María Soledad Quiroga (Santiago, Chile, 1957) has been a columnist for several newspapers in La Paz. After having studied literature at the Universidad Mayor de San Andrés in La Paz, and professional studies in education, environmental development, local development, and multiculturalism, she received a degree in sociology from the Universidad Nacional Autónoma de México. She was Minister of Education, 2004-2005 and published over thirty articles on educational and environmental themes, including *Figuras, rostros, máscaras: las identidades en Bolivia*, a study on national identification and intercultural issues. .

In 2004, María Soledad Quiroga was awarded the "Gran Oficial" Cultural and Educational Order of Merit "Gabriela Mistral," from the Republic of Chile, and in 2006, she received the order of "Oficial" of the Palmas Académicas from the Ministry of Education of France. Her poems and short stories have appeared in eight national and international anthologies, as well as in literature textbooks for secondary schools in Bolivia. In 2006 she published *Islas reunión*, a collection of short stories. She currently resides in La Paz and works as a consultant for various organizations.

POETRY

Ciudad blanca. La Paz: PAP, 1993.
Recuento del agua. La Paz: Plural, 1995.
Maquinaria mínima. La Paz: Plural, 1995.
Casa amarilla. La Paz: Plural, 1998.
Los muros del claustro. La Paz: Plural, 2004.
Traza de caracol. La Paz: Plural, 2011.

Poems in Spanish of Marisol Quiroga can be found online at:

"Antología antojadiza sobre poética de mujeres de América." Apr. 2011.
http://conestebocaenestemundo.blogspot.com/

CRITICISM, REVIEWS, INTERVIEWS

Bajo, R. "María Soledad Quiroga y la tentación." *Fondo Negro (La Prensa*, La Paz) 6 June 2004: 4-5.

Contreras, Pilar and Elías Blanco. *Existencias insurrectas. La mujer en la cultura*. La Paz: Subsecretaría de Asuntos de Género, Agenda Gesta de Servicio Informativo Cultural. La Paz, Bolivia, 1997.

García, Mara Lucy. *Escritoras bolivianas de hoy*. Santa Cruz, Bolivia: La Hoguera, 2008.

Haladyna, Ronald. "La provocativa poesía de María Soledad Quiroga." *Nueva Crónica (Prisma y Plural*, La Paz) 56 (12-25 Feb. 2010) 16-17.

Hill, Matthew J.K. "Quiroga, María Soledad. *Islas reunión.*" *Chasqui* 38.1 (2009): 209.

"El lenguaje del cuerpo: la trayectoria del cuerpo." *Memoria del Coloquio 'El cuerpo en los imaginarios.'* La Paz: Espacio Simón I. Patiño; Carrera de Literatura de la Universidad Mayor de San Andrés; Departamento de Arte y Cultura de la Universidad Católica Boliviana San Pablo, 2003.

Leonard, Kathy, ed. "Una revelación desde la escritura.*" Entrevistas a poetas bolivianas*. New York: Peter Lang, 2001.

Mac Lean, Juan Cristóbal. "Entrega de piedras." *Pulso* (La Paz, Bolivia) 10 Sep. 2004.

Mitre, Eduardo. *El aliento en las hojas: Otras voces en la poesía boliviana*. La Paz: Plural, 1998.

—. "'La literatura es siempre invento,' dice María Soledad Quiroga." Interview with "K." 23 Nov. 2007: http://culpinak.blogspot. com/2007/11/la-literatura-es-siempre-invento-dice.html

—. "Sobre *Casa amarilla.*" *Memoria / Encuentro Diálogos sobre Escritura y Mujeres*. Ed. and selection: Ana Rebeca Prada, Virginia Ayllón y Pilar Contreras. Taller Ayllón, Bruzonic, Contreras, Gutiérrez, Prada, Selum, Embajada Real de los Países Bajos, La Paz, Bolivia. 1999.

Teixidó, Raúl. "Con voz propia." *Puño y letra (Correo del Sur*, Sucre, Bolivia) 20 Jan. 2007.

Vargas, Rubén. "Apuntes sobre *Los muros del claustro* de María Soledad Quiroga." (Unpublished text pronounced during the presentation of Ms. Quiroga's book.) La Paz, Bolivia, 2004.

Velásquez G., Mónica. *Ordenar la danza. Antología de la poesía boliviana.* Santiago, Chile: LOM, 2004.

—. "Entre el exterior y la interioridad: la palabra caracol de María Soledad Quiroga." *Nueva Crónica* (*Prisma y Plural*, La Paz) 85 (May 2011) 17.

—. "Los rumores del mundo. A propósito de *Ciudad Blanca* de María Soledad Quiroga." *Presencia Literaria* (La Paz) 23 May 1993.

****

FERNANDO ROSSO

A poet in life, as well as in his works, Rosso (Sucre, Bolivia, 1945) studied law, but never practiced it. He resided for years in Tarija, but currently lives and rides his bicycle in Cochabamba.

POETRY

El danzante y la muerte. La Paz: Altiplano, 1983; La Paz: Artes Gráficas Sagitario, 2003; 2nd. ed. La Paz: Hombrecito Sentado /Plural, 2004.

Aire hereje. La Paz: Author's ed., 1986.

Parte de copas. La Paz: Ojo Libertario, 1989.

Los días. La Paz: Author's ed. 1995.

El eje de las horas. La Paz: AGP de Luxe, 2007.

CRITICISM, REVIEWS, INTERVIEWS

Arauz, G. "Escritores en su tinta." *La Razón* (La Paz) 4 Apr. 1992: B8.

Guerra, A. "Parte de copas." Review. *Opinión* (Cochabamba) 19 Oct. 1989: 2.

Quirós, J. "El danzante y la muerte." Review *Signo* 12 (1984): 248-249.

Rosso, F. "Poemas de Fernando Rosso." *Presencia Literaria* (La Paz)
8 May 1994: 10.

****

PEDRO SHIMOSE

A self-taught poet and literary critic, Pedro Shimose (Riberalta, Beni,
Bolivia, 1940) worked in La Paz as a journalist for *Presencia* and as a
professor of literature at the Universidad Mayor San Andrés. He has
lived in Madrid since 1972, where he carries out research on literary
themes for the Instituto de Cooperación Iberoamericana.

Shimose won the Casa de las Américas literary award in 1972 for his
book *Quiero escribir, pero me sale espuma*, and the National Prize
for Culture in 1999. His work in bibliography, criticism, and history
are also notable: *Diccionario de autores iberoamericanos* (1982);
Historia de la literatura latinoamericana, (1989; second edition,
1993); *Literatura hispanoamericana actual* (1993); a book on poet
Álvaro Mutis; and a book of short stories, *El coco se llama drilo*
(1976). Shimose keeps in touch with his heritage through annual visits
to Bolivia and he still writes occasional columns for the newspaper
El Deber in Santa Cruz de la Sierra.

POETRY

Triludio en el exilio. La Paz: Signo, 1961.
Sardonia. La Paz: UMSA, 1967.
Poemas para un pueblo. La Paz: Difusión, 1968.
Quiero escribir pero me sale espuma. Havana, Cuba: Casa de las
    Américas, 1972.
Poemas / Pedro Shimose. Prologue Teodosio Fernández. Madrid:
    Playor, 1988.
Caducidad del fuego. Madrid: Cultura Hispánica, 1975. 2nd ed. Santa
    Cruz de la Sierra: El País, 2005.
Al pie de la letra. Jaén, Spain: Diego Sánchez del Real D.L., 1976.
Reflexiones maquiavélicas. Madrid, Spain: Playor, 1980; 4th ed.
    Santa Cruz de la Sierra: El País, 2003.

Bolero de caballería. Madrid: Playor, 1985.

Poemas. Madrid: Playor, 1988.

Bolero der Chevalerie. [Trans. of *Bolero de Caballería*] Stuttgart, Germany: Delta, 1994.

Riberalta y otros poemas. Santa Cruz de la Sierra: El País, 1996.

No te lo vas a creer. Santa Cruz de la Sierra: El País, 2000; Rprt. Madrid: Verbum, 2001.

De naufragios y sonámbulos: antología poética. Santa Cruz de la Sierra, Bolivia: El País, 2003.

[With Se-Yong O and Changmin Kim] *Sueños del barranco: Antología.* Madrid, Spain: Verbum, 2003.

Riflessioni machiavelliche. Trans. Claudio Cinti. Venice, Italy: Sinopia Libri, 2004.

Quiero escribir pero me sale espuma. 2nd. ed. Santa Cruz: El País, 2004.

A selection of poems by Pedro Shimose can be found online at: http://www.boliviaweb.com/poetry/shimose.htm

CRITICISM, REVIEWS, INTERVIEWS

Baciu, S. "Pedro Shimose." *Presencia Literaria* (29 Aug. 1993): 16.

Bolivian Studies. La Paz: Instituto de Estudios Bolivianos, 1990.

Bornstein, Miriam Mijalina. "Nueva poesía socio-política: La Expresión hispana." *DAI* 43.7 (1983): 2358A.

Chávez Taborga, César. *Shimose, poeta en cuatro estaciones.* Mérida, Venezuela: Centro de Investigaciones Literarias Universidad de los Andes, 1974.

Clifford, Joan. *Modern Spanish American Poets. First Series.* Ed. Salgado, María Antonia. Detroit, MI: Gale Group, 2003.

De la Vega, Julio. "Del surrealismo a lo social en la poesía boliviana." *El paseo de los sentidos.* Eds. Leonardo García Pabón and Wilma Torrico. La Paz: Instituto Boliviano de Cultura, 1983. 3-33.

Gumucio Dagrón, Alfonso. "Los resortes de la libertad. Pedro Shimose, Premio Poesía Casa de las Américas." *Marcha* (Montevideo) 12 May 1972: 30-31.

Herrera, Ricardo. "Shimose y Baptista Gumucio. Diálogo y amistad." *El Deber* (Santa Cruz de la Sierra, Bolivia) 3 July 2007:http://www.eldeber.com.bo/anteriores/20030405/escenas_9.html

Hurtado Suárez, O. G. *Pedro Shimose y su obra.* Trinidad: Universidad Boliviana José Ballivián, 1976.

Iffland, James. "Pedro Shimose en sus reflexiones maquiavélicas." *Hispanófila* 129 (2000): 75-98.

Lee, Debbie. "When East Meets West: An Examination of the Poetry of the Asian Diaspora in Spanish America." Diss. U of Missouri-Columbia, 2001. *DAI* 62.4 (2001): 1433.

Mijalina Bornstein, Miriam. "Nueva poesía socio-política: La expresión hispana." *DAI:* 43.7 (1983): 2358A.

Mitre, Eduardo. "Cuatro poetas bolivianos contemporáneos." *Revista Iberoamericana* 52.134 (1986): 139-163.

—. "Del fervor al escepticismo: La poesía de Pedro Shimose." *Cuadernos Hispanoamericanos* 438 (1986): 147-153; Rprt. *El paseo de los sentidos.* Ed. Leonardo García Pabón and Wilma Torrico. La Paz: Instituto Boliviano de Cultura, 1983. 129-136.

Ortega, José. *Letras bolivianas de hoy: Renato Prada y Pedro Shimose.* Buenos Aires: Fernando García Cambeiro, 1973.

—. *Renato Prada y P. Shimose: Escritores bolivianos de nuestro tiempo.* Buenos Aires: Estudios Latinoamericanos, 1973.

—. "Exilio boliviano." *Hispamérica* 1.3 (1973): 46-68.

—. "Pedro Shimose, poeta comprometido." *La Palabra y el hombre.* (Universidad Veracruzana) 13 (1975): 63-68.

—. "Pedro Shimose, poeta comprometido." *XVII Congreso del Instituto Internacional de Literatura Iberoamericana: El barroco en América; Literatura hispanoamericana; Crítica histórico-literaria hispanoamericana.* Madrid: Cultura Hispánica del Centro Iberoamericano de Cooperación, Univ. Complutense de Madrid, 1978. 897-907.

Poeta Movima. *Literary Amazonia: Modern Writing by Amazonian Authors.* Gainesville, FL: UP of Florida, 2004.

Quirós, Juan. "Panorama de la poesía en Bolivia." *Los ensayistas: Georgia Series on Hispanic Thought.* 20-21 (1986): 221-241.

Roca, José Luis. Nota preliminar. *Sardonia.* By Pedro Shimose. La Paz: Universidad Mayor de San Andrés, 1967.

Rozas, Juan M. "Encuentro con Pedro Shimose, premio de poesía Casa de las Américas." *Ínsula: Revista de Letras y Ciencias Humanas* 27 (1972): 4-5.

Salgado, María A. "Una lectura maquiavélica de Pedro Shimose." *Revista Hispánica Moderna* 48.2 (1995): 349-64.

Sanjinés, C. "Pedro Shimose: Poeta rebelde e intelectual letrado." *RLA: Romance Languages Annual* 4 (1992) 570-74.

Shimose, Pedro. *Renato Prada y Pedro Shimose: Escritores bolivianos de nuestro tiempo.*" Buenos Aires: Estudios Latinoamericanos, 1973.

—. "Pedro Shimose, poeta comprometido." *La palabra y el hombre: Revista de la Universidad Veracruzana.* 13 (1975): 63-68.

—. "Pedro Shimose, poeta comprometido." XVII Congreso del Instituto International de Literatura Iberoamericana: El barroco en América; Literatura hispanoamericana; Crítica histórico-literaria hispanoamericana. Madrid: 1978. 897-907.

—. "De cerca: Pedro Shimose, Pablo Solón y Gil Imana." Interview with Carlos D. Mesa (Periodista Asociados de Televisión). La Paz: P.A.T., 1992-1998. DVD, 102 mins.

—. "Entrevista con Pedro Shimose." Interview with Alberto Julián Pérez. *Alba de América: Revista Literaria* 11.20-21 (1993): 497-501.

—. "Entrevista con Pedro Shimose." Interview with Debbie Lee. *PALARA* (Afro-Latin/American Research Association) 4 (2000): 84-89.

—. "Pedro Shimose." Interview with Alfonso Gumucio Dagrón. *Provocaciones.* Ed. Alfonso Gumucio Dagrón. 2nd. ed. La Paz: Plural, 2006.

Sisson, Michael Drew. "Intertextuality in the Poetry of Pedro Shimose." *DAI* 55.6 (1994): 1575A.

Whittingham, Georgina J. and Rachelle Moore. "La relación lenguaje-historia: Poscolonialismo y posmodernidad en *Poemas para un pueblo* y *Caducidad del fuego* de Pedro Shimose." Ed. Silvia Elguea Véjar. *La otredad: Los discursos de la cultura hoy, 1995.* Mexico City: Universidad Autónoma Metropolitana-A., 1997. 275-96.

Wiethüchter, Blanca. "Poesía contemporánea: Oscaro Cerruto, Jaime Sáenz, Pedro Shimose, Jesús Urzagasti." *Tendencias actuales en la literatura boliviana.* Ed. and Intro. Javier Sanjinés C. Minneapolis: Institute for the Study of Ideologies and Literature / Instituto de Cine & Radio Televisión, 1985. 75-114.

****

VILMA TAPIA

Vilma Tapia (La Paz, 1960) received a degree in education from the Universidad Mayor de San Simón de Cochabamba, and has lived in the city ever since. She later did post-graduate work in relational dimensions of human systems in Santiago, Chile, and then returned to Cochabamba to get a degree in community mental health. She has worked in education, journalism, and rural development. She has edited and collaborated in various literary reviews, has conducted workshops in creative writing, and has been a guest participant in poetry festivals in Latin American and Europe. Articles of hers have appeared in various news media and reviews in Bolivia, Colombia, Spain, Portugal, Belgium, and Austria.

Ms. Tapia's poems have been included in *Antología de la poesía viva en Bolivia* (2001), *Antología de la poesía boliviana* (2004), and the bilingual anthology (Spanish-German) *Poesía entre dos mundos* (2004),

POETRY

Del deseo y la rosa. Cochabamba/La Paz: Los Amigos del Libro, 1992.
Corazones de terca escama. La Paz: Hombrecito Sentado / Plural, 1995; 2nd. ed., Hombrecito Sentado/Plural, 2004.
Oh estaciones, oh castillos. La Paz: Hombrecito sentado, 1999.
Luciérnagas del fondo. La Paz: Plural, 2003.
La fiesta de mi boda. La Paz: Plural, 2006.
El agua más cercana. La Paz: Gente Común, 2008.

For easy access to some of Vilma Tapia's poems in Spanish, see:
http://quipusl.com/poesiaenparalelelocero/Vilma-Tapia.php

CRITICISM, REVIEWS, INTERVIEWS

Martins, Floriano. "Dos poetas bolivianos: Vilma Tapia Anaya y
    Gary Daher Canedo." *Revista Agulha* (Fortaleza-São Paolo,
    Brazil) March-April 2006 :http://www.revista.agulha. nom.
    br/ag50martins.htm
—. *Escritura conquistada: conversaciones con poetas de
    Latinoamérica.* Caracas, Venezuela: Ministerio del Poder
    Popular para la Cultura; Fundación Editorial El Perro y la
    Rana, 2009.
Mitre, Eduardo. "Del espejo de la alcoba a la plaza." *Alejandría*
    (La Paz) May 2008: 12-14.
Terán, Antonio. "Vilma entregó libro." *Opinión* (17 July 1992): 10.
Torre, L. [No title.] *Boletín Literario* (Fundación Patiño,
    Cochabamba) 5 (2004): 6-9.
Vanello, Daniel. "Tapia y el posible eclecticismo coherente." *Los
    Tiempos.com* (Edición Semanal, Cochabamba, Bolivia)
    26 Nov. 2006. http://www.lostiempos.com/lecturas/26-11-
    06/26_11_06_arte3.php
Velásquez, Mónica. "De la celebración y la serenidad. Rev. of *Fiesta
    de mi boda*, by Vilma Tapia. *Alejandría* 7 (2006): 15.
—. "En torno a la poesía de Vilma Tapia Anaya" *Presencia Literaria*
    (La Paz) 2 Jun. 1996.
Zelada Cabrera, Michel. "Tapia baila con la palabra en *La fiesta de
    mi boda*." *Los Tiempos*.com (Cochabamba, Bolivia.) 1 Nov.
    2006: http://www.lostiempos.com/noticias/01 11 06/tragaluz.
    php
Zurita, Raúl. "Preferible amar de amor." *Oh estaciones, oh castillos*.
    By Vilma Tapia. La Paz: Hombrecito sentado, 1999. 3-4.

****

ANTONIO TERÁN CABERO

Poet and literary critic, Antonio Terán Cabero (Cochabamba, 1932) studied law, but never practiced it. Instead, he occupied many posts in the municipal government of Cochabamba, including that of assistant mayor, and director of the Department of Culture. For many years he was a specialist in urban planning, and his retirement in 2000 permitted him to devote himself full time to poetry. Terán "el soldado" (the soldier), is a recognized composer of sonnets, and belongs to the second generation of the "Gesta Barba," a literary movement that included Jacobo Libermann, Julio de la Vega, Jorge Suárez and Gustavo Medinacelli. Terán won the national prize for poetry in 2003 "Premio Nacional de Poesía Yolanda Bedregal," for his book *Boca abajo y murciélago*. He still resides in Cochabamba.

POETRY

Puerto imposible. Cochabamba, Bolivia: Canelas, 1963.
Y negarse a morir. Cochabamba, Bolivia: Universitaria, 1979.
Bajo el ala del sombrero. Cochabamba: Universitaria, 1989.
Ahora que es entonces. Cochabamba: Portales, 1993.
De aquel umbral sediento: Sonetos. Cochabamba: M y C, 1998.
Boca abajo y murciélago—otras palabras al acecho. La Paz: Plural, 2004.

CRITICISM, REVIEWS, INTERVIEWS

Aries. "Antonio Terán Cabero: Navegante en el proceloso mar de la poesía." *Presencia Literaria* (La Paz) 5 May 1996: 8-10
—. "La poesía de Antonio Terán." *Suplemento Literario* (*El País*, Santa Cruz de la Sierra) 6 (27 Apr. 1980): 8.
Ávila Echazú, Édgar. [No title.] Antonio Terán Cabero. *De aquel umbral sediento*. Cochabamba: M & C, 1998. Back cover.
Castañón, C. "De aquel umbral sediento." *Signo* 51/52 (1999): 371.
Quinteros Soria, Juan. "En el universo del poeta Antonio Terán Cabero: 'Ahora que es entonces.'" *Presencia Literaria* (La Paz) 9 Mar. 1997: 1-4.

—. "La poesía del vate Antonio Terán Cabero." *Opinión* Cochabamba, 9 Jul. 1985): 9.

Quiroga, Giancarla de. "La poesía de Antonio Terán Cabero." *Presencia Literaria* (La Paz, 18 Apr. 1993): 3.

Quiroga, Igor. "Antonio Terán Cabero: El Puente." *Correo Cultural* (*Los Tiempos*, Cochabamba) 61 (1987): 1-4.

Suárez, Jorge S. [No title.] Antonio Terán Cabero. *Puerto imposible.* Cochabamba, Bolivia: Canelas, 1963. Inside front and back covers.

Terán, Antonio. "Esta herida." *Presencia Literaria* (La Paz) 16.3 (1986): 1.

Vargas, Rubén. [No title.] *Boca abajo y murciélago—y otras palabras al acecho.* By Antonio Terán Cabero. La Paz: Plural, 2004. Back cover.

****

MÓNICA VELÁSQUEZ

Poet, essayist, literary critic and professor of poetry, world literature, research methodology, and of creative writing at the Universidad Mayor de San Andrés (UMSA), Mónica Velásquez (La Paz, 1972) has devoted her life to literature. After completing her Bachelor's degree in literature at the UMSA, she went on to earn her M. A. and her Ph.D. at the Colegio de México in 2004. She has written numerous essays, reviews and books on Latin American poets and narrative writers, including: *Antología de poesía boliviana del siglo XX: Ordenar la danza* (2004); coordination of a monograph devoted to Bolivia for the Portuguese literary review, *Nuestra América 3* (2007); *Obra poética completa* (of Bolivian poet Oscar Cerruto); *Múltiples voces en la poesía de Francisco Hernández, Blanca Wiethüchter y Raúl Zurita* (2009); and *Demoniaco afán: ensayos sobre poesía latinoamericana* (2011). Mónica Velásquez was awarded Bolivia's Premio Nacional de Poesía Yolanda Bedregal in 2007 for her book *Hija de Medea*.

POETRY

Tres nombres para un lugar. La Paz:Hombrecito Sentado, 1995; 2nd.
   ed. La Paz: Hombrecito Sentado / Plural: 2004.
Fronteras de doble filo. La Paz: Plural, 1998.
El viento de los náufragos. La Paz: Plural, 2005.
Hija de Medea. La Paz: Plural, 2008.

For an online selection of poems in Spanish of Mónica Velásquez,
   see: http://www.bolivianet.com/poetas/velasquez.html

CRITICISM, REVIEWS, INTERVIEWS

Mitre, Eduardo. "Padre, ¿por qué nunca me has abandonado?"
   Primera Revista Latinoamericana de Libros PRL June-July,
   2008.
Vega, Julio de la. [No title]. *Fronteras de doble filo.* By Mónica
   Velásquez. La Paz: Plural, 1999. Back cover.
—. "Nuevo libro de poesia." *Semana* (*Última Hora*, La Paz) 21 Jan.
   2006.
Velásquez, Mónica. Interview with Kathy Leonard. *Una revelación
   desde la escritura: entrevistas a poetas bolivianas*, New
   York: Peter Lang, 2001. Also, see: http://www.lostiempos.
   com/noticias/23-02-08/23_02_08_trag1.php
—. "Entrevista a Mónica Velásquez Guzmán." Interview with
   Javier Claure Covarrubias. *Panorama Cultural* (Stockholm,
   Sweden, 3 June 2008):http://www.panoramacultural.
   net/Suecia/mPaginas/pSelectRecord.cfm?paginaID
   =1587&CategoriaID=61

****

BLANCA WIETHÜCHTER

With a degree in literature from the Universidad Mayor de San
Andrés (La Paz), another in Education from the Université de la
Sorbonne (Paris), a Master's in Spanish American Literature from
the Université de Paris, and a Diplome d'Études Approfondies

from the Sorbonne Nouvelle, Blanca Wiethüchter (La Paz, 1947-Cochabamba, 2004) demonstrated in the 1970s a passion for learning that would carry over to her teaching, research and writing. She taught Spanish American and other literature courses for many years at the Universidad Mayor de San Andrés and at the Universidad Católica, and also was coordinator and director of literature programs at these and other institutions of higher learning in La Paz.

At the same time Ms. Wiethüchter was very active in editorial work, having collaborated in literary reviews—*Revista Hipótesis, Revista Piedra Imán,* and *Hormiga Eléctrica* (cultural supplement of *La Razón*), as well as on the editorial staff of publishers such as Altiplano, Hombrecito Sentado, Mujercita Sentada, and Parejita Sentada. She published three monographs of literary history and criticism: *Las estructuras de lo imaginario en la obra poética de Jaime Sáenz* (1975); *Los melancólicos senderos del tiempo: Pérez Alcalá* (1997); co-authored and co-directed *Hacia una historia crítica de la literatura en Bolivia* (2002); and together with Fernando Rosso, she wrote *La geografía suena: Biografía crítica de Alberto Villalpando,* a study of the works of her husband, composer Alberto Villalpando.

She also wrote and published numerous reviews and studies on contemporary literature, especially on Bolivian poetry, co-authored *Hacia una historia crítica de la literature en Bolivia* and three editions of her memoirs *Memoria solicitada.* In spite of all of these activities, she was still able to write numerous books of poetry, narrative literature, scripts for videos, and a theatrical work.

POETRY

Asistir al tiempo. La Paz: Author's ed., 1975.
Travesía. La Paz: Author's ed., 1978.
Noviembre 79. La Paz: Piedra Libre, 1979.
Bolivian poet Blanca Wiethüchter reading from her work. [Audio-book. Archive of Hispanic Literature on Tape (Library of Congress), 1980.
Madera viva y árbol difunto. La Paz: Altiplano, 1982.
Territorial. La Paz: Altiplano, 1983.

En los negros labios encantados. Santa Cruz: Altiplano, 1989.

El verde no es un color. La Paz: El Hombrecito Sentado, 1992; 2nd. ed. La Paz: Hombrecito Sentado / Plural, 2004.

El rigor de la llama. Cochabamba: Centro Simón I. Patiño, 1994.

La lagarta. 2nd. ed. La Paz: Hombrecito Sentado, 1995.

Sayariy. (Poems for the motion picture by the same name.) La Paz: Hombrecito Sentado, 1996.

Qantatai. La Paz: El Hombrecito Sentado, 1998.

El jardín de Nora. La Paz: El Hombrecito Sentado, 1998.

La piedra que labra otra piedra. (Anthology.) La Paz: Hombrecito Sentado, 1998.

Itaca. La Paz: El Hombrecito Sentado, 2000.

Ítaca; Ángeles del miedo; madera viva, árbol difunto. La Paz: UMSA / Gente Común, 2004.

Ángeles del miedo. La Paz: El Hombrecito Sentado / Plural, 2005.

Assistere al tempo. Venice, Italy: Sinopia, 2005.

Luminar. La Paz: Hombrecito Sentado / Plural, 2005.

No se mira hacia arriba se mira hacia abajo. La Paz: Fundación Simón I. Patiño / Plural, 2007.

A selection of Blanca Wiethüchter's poetry can be found at: http://www.palabravirtual.com/index.php?ir=crit.php&wid=631&show=poemas&p=Blanca+Wieth%FCchter http://www.boliviaweb.com/poetry/wiethuchter.htm

CRITICISM, REVIEWS, INTERVIEWS

García Pabón, Leonardo. "Penélope does not wait anymore: On the late poetry of Blanca Wiethüchter." Conference paper. International Conference on Women, Gender and discourse in Latin America. Liverpool, United Kingdom. 2 Mar. 2007

Mitre, Eduardo. *El aliento en las hojas: Otras voces de la poesía boliviana.* La Paz: Plural, 1998.

Monasterios, Elizabeth. *Poesía boliviana contemporánea: hacia la comprensión del imaginario poético en la obra de Blanca Wiethüchter.* [M.A. dissertation.] Ottawa: National Library of Canada, 1990.

—. *Latin American Narratives and Cultural Identity: Selected Readings*. Ed. Irene Maria F. Blayer and Mark Cronlund Anderson. New York: Peter Lang, 2004. 94-110.

Ordóñez, Montserrat. "La poesía de Blanca Wiethüchter." *Revista Iberoamericana* 52.134 (1986): 197-206.

Reinaga Campos, Lucía Tijsi. *De las montañas de la locura a las montañas de La Paz: el hueco como herramienta para leer horror en la ficción*. La Paz: Universidad Mayor de San Andres, Instituto de Estudios bolivianos, 2008.

Richmond, Blanca A. *Structuralist literary criticism in action: A Bolivian model: Blanca Wiethüchter's Bolivian Contemporary Poetry: Oscar Cerruto, Jaime Saenz, Pedro Shimose, Jesús Urzagasti: Translation and Commentary*. [M. A. Thesis.] Grand Forks, N.D.: University of North Dakota, 1991.

Sanjinés C., Javier. [No title.] *La lagarta*. La Paz: Hombrecito Sentado, 1995. 5-6.

Velásquez, Mónica. "Los caminos del 'yo' en la poesía de Blanca Wiethüchter." *La piedra que labra otra piedra: Poesía*. La Paz: Hombrecito Sentado, 1998. 5-11.

—. "Voces y búsqueda en la poesía de Blanca Wiethüchter." *Al Pie de la Letra* (*Hoy*, La Paz) 18 Jan. 1998.

—. *Polifonía poética*. La Paz: Univ. Mayor de San Andrés,1999.

—. "Recordar sólo lo que hace vivir." *Blanca Wiethüchter o el lugar del fuego*. Ed. Marcelo Villena. La Paz: Gente Común / UMSA, 2004.

—. "Si Ítaca fuera la muerte (extrañando a B. Wiethüchter)." *Tinkazos* 18 (2005).

—. *Múltiples voces en la poesía de Francisco Hernández, Blanca Wiethüchter y Raúl Zurita*. Mexico City: El Colegio de México, 2009.

Villena Alvarado, Marcelo, ed. *Blanca Wiethüchter, el lugar del fuego*. La Paz: UMSA / Gente Común, 2004.

—. "Réquiem para un modelo: Hueco y experiencia literaria en la obra de Blanca Wiethüchter." *Les Modèles et leur circulation en Amérique latine: Modèles et structures du roman; Révision es stéréotypes; Transfer de modèles*. Ed. François Delprat. Paris France : Sorbonne Nouvelle, 2006. 157-65.

Wiethüchter, Blanca. "De cerca: Carlos Villagómez, Carlos

Ormachea y Blanca Wiethüchter." Interview with Carlos D. Mesa. La Paz: P.A.T. (Periodistas Asociados de Televisión. 1987-2000. DVD. 123 mins.

—. "Entrevista con Blanca Wiethüchter." Interview with Alberto Julián Pérez. *Alba de América: Revista Literaria*. 11:20-21 (1993): 481-487.

—. "Entrevista con Matilde Casazola Mendoza y Blanca Wiethüchter." Interview with Kathy S. Leonard. *Bolivian Studies*, 8 (2000): 58-128.

—. *El rigor de la llama: Blanca Wiethüchter, una entrevista.* Interview with Leonardo García Pabón. (DVD video) La Paz: Plural, 2006.

****

ABOUT THE EDITOR

Ronald Haladyna is professor emeritus of Spanish and Latin American Culture at Ferris State University in Big Rapids, Michigan. His experience in Latin America is extensive and diverse: Peace Corps Volunteer in Cusco, Peru (1967-69); professor of English at the Universidad Autónoma del Estado de México (Toluca, 1974-84); senior Fulbright researcher and lecturer in Asunción, Paraguay (1997); and a recipient of sabbatical leaves and research grants (1997-2008) to carry out research in Paraguay, Uruguay, Ecuador, and Bolivia.

Author of numerous articles, papers, and several books on Latin American poetry, he also is co-translator of Paraguayan poet Renée Ferrer's *Sobreviviente / Survivor* (1999); and has compiled and edited *Contemporary Uruguayan Poetry: A Bilingual Anthology* (2010); *Exotic Territory: A Bilingual Anthology of Contemporary Paraguayan Poetry* (2011); and *Volcanic Reflections: A Bilingual Anthology of Contemporary Ecuadorian Poetry* (2011). Dr. Haladyna resides on a nature preserve in Big Rapids, Michigan.